Mastering the Art
of Teaching

Mastering the Art of Teaching

Meeting the Challenges of the Multidimensional, Multifaceted Tasks of Today's Classrooms

Selma Wassermann

ROWMAN & LITTLEFIELD
Lanham • Boulder • New York • London

Published by Rowman & Littlefield
An imprint of The Rowman & Littlefield Publishing Group, Inc.
4501 Forbes Boulevard, Suite 200, Lanham, Maryland 20706
www.rowman.com

6 Tinworth Street, London SE11 5AL, United Kingdom

Copyright © 2021 by Selma Wassermann

All rights reserved. No part of this book may be reproduced in any form or by any electronic or mechanical means, including information storage and retrieval systems, without written permission from the publisher, except by a reviewer who may quote passages in a review.

British Library Cataloguing in Publication Information Available

Library of Congress Cataloging-in-Publication Data

Names: Wassermann, Selma, author.
Title: Mastering the art of teaching : meeting the challenges of the multi-dimensional, multi-faceted tasks of today's classrooms / Selma Wassermann.
Description: Lanham, Maryland : Rowman & Littlefield, 2021. | Includes bibliographical references and index. | Summary: "The book not only identifies and explains what teachers do but also makes suggestions for new and practicing teachers may further hone those skills that each task demands"—Provided by publisher.
Identifiers: LCCN 2020042777 (print) | LCCN 2020042778 (ebook) | ISBN 9781475858648 (cloth) | ISBN 9781475858655 (paperback) | ISBN 9781475858662 (epub)
Subjects: LCSH: Teaching. | First year teachers. | Teachers—In-service training. | Teacher-student relationships.
Classification: LCC LB1025.3 .W376 2021 (print) | LCC LB1025.3 (ebook) | DDC 371.102—dc23
LC record available at https://lccn.loc.gov/2020042777
LC ebook record available at https://lccn.loc.gov/2020042778

For Paula, my darling girl

Contents

Preface		xi
Acknowledgments		xvii
Introduction		xix
1	Scenes from a Classroom	1
	The Teacher as Decision Maker	3
2	Beginnings	5
	What's Wrong with Teacher Education?	6
	Some Advice for "Noo Teechrs"	8
	Last Words	9
3	The Professional Tasks of the Teacher	11
	The Development of an Assessment Instrument to Evaluate Teaching Competence	12
	Profiles of Teaching Competency	12
	Categories of Teaching Competency	13
4	Teacher as Person	15
	Growing Teachers	16
	Being Clear about What's Important	16
	Sharpening Your Problem-Solving Skills	18
	The Importance of Being Real	20
	Developing Confidence in Self	22
	Taking Care of Yourself	24
	Conclusion	24

5	**The Teacher and the Kids**	27
	Teacher as Diagnostician	28
	Identifying Students Showing Extreme Emotional Needs	30
	Teaching Strategies for Dealing with Emotional Needs	32
	Identifying Behavior that Relates to Lack of Experience with Thinking	34
	Teaching Strategies for Dealing with Lack of Experience with Thinking	35
	Other Behavior Impediments to Learning	38
	Conclusion	38
6	**Teacher-Student Interactions**	41
	It Starts with Listening, Attending, and Apprehending	44
	Choosing the Right Response	46
	Mastering the Art of Teacher-Student Interactions	54
	Conclusion	55
7	**The Teacher and the Curriculum**	57
	IT and the Curriculum	58
	A Few Examples of Existing School Programs Incorporating IT	60
	What Can a Teacher Do?	63
	Putting the Teaching for Thinking Curriculum Framework into Practice	68
	Why Do These Students Love School?	71
8	**Evaluation as a Tool for Improving Learning**	73
	Creating More Effective Assessment Tools	73
	Diagnosing Students' Difficulties	76
	Giving Evaluative Feedback	77
	Students' Self-Evaluations	79
	Reporting to Parents	80
	Conclusion	81
9	**Teaching as a Courageous Activity**	83
	The Closed Classroom Door	84
	Teachers Who Dared	85
10	**What's the Payoff?**	91
	What's in It for Me?	92
11	**Endpaper**	95
	A Personal Journey	95

Appendix	99
Bibliography	125
Index	129
About the Author	133

Preface

Like many of you readers, I have had a few master teachers in my life, and I am blessed to have had my life enriched by them. The teaching strategies they used and the classroom experiences we had were heads and shoulders above and beyond what I had experienced before, and that was obvious from the very first day. There was an ethos in those classrooms that "spoke" to me as well—a sense that we students were a community of learners and that what was on offer was special. There are many good reasons that these teachers are remembered and held in such high regard.

When I was introduced to the importance of teacher-student interactions and their effect on student learning, I would, in a free period, sit in on Louis Raths's classes—not to hear, again, what he had to say about students' needs, values, and thinking but to watch him as he listened, questioned, interacted respectfully with each student, always with an ear to the importance of what each was saying. He made each of us feel as if we were partners in learning, together exploring ideas that would illuminate our thinking and our understanding. Watching him was like being in a master class. I was studying the "master" and trying to bring some of those teaching strategies into accord with my own.

Coming to an appreciation of how case method teaching could be a useful curriculum tool for promoting student thinking and awareness of critical issues in subject areas, I sat in "Chris" Christensen's classes at the Harvard Business School, observing and studying the way he "taught" a case. Once again, his respect for every student in that class was manifest; his questions, probing, insightful, clarifying. He seemed to know when to question, when to reflect, when to probe, when to confront. The students seemed rapt in attention, listening, carefully forming their own responses to his queries. His orchestration of a class discussion I compared to Toscanini conducting the

New York Philharmonic, and I left his classes on a high, better aware of the superior skills of teacher-student interactions. This was teaching at the highest level of art.

Dr. Ed Lipinksi was the chief medical officer and psychiatrist in the Health Services division of the university where I taught for many years. He took me in hand and gave me two years of tutorials in counselling, where I sharpened my skills as a respectful listener, and more important, learned to make thoughtful and insightful diagnosis into human behavior, which led to more effective interventions in dealing with presenting problems. He was patient and kind, and he knew when to ask and when to advise. His knowledge of human behavior and counselling interventions gave me deeper insights into the rationale for why some humans behave as they do.

Not every teacher is, in fact, a teacher by profession. There are a few masters outside of the profession who do teach and whose lessons have great impact. On one sabbatical, I wormed my way into the lives of a group of bakers, to learn more about the process of producing high-quality French pastry. I spent two weeks sweating in front of the ovens of Fantasia Bakery in South San Francisco, where I began my apprenticeship by being allowed to shape the dough of croissants that were just ready to go into the ovens. About eight hundred of them each morning.

Being new and utterly without experience, I turned the edges of each piece of dough upward, doing this again and again over a series of giant-size baking pans. One of the bakers looked at my work and, instead of admonishing, or chastising, or berating, smiled and showed me that if those dough ends went into the ovens turned up, instead of down, the croissants would not lie flat but instead come out as if they had wings. He demonstrated the correct way and guided my hands in repairing the first hundred croissants so that I could learn the technique correctly.

It was a lesson in graceful feedback after having committed what could have been an egregious error. You just can't toss 800 croissants into the bin when they come out of the oven in the wrong shape. The ovens were already scheduled for the next batch of pastries.

Despite my ignorance and hopeless lack of experience in a bakery, the bakers were generous in allowing me to undertake more complicated and challenging tasks, always at the ready to help when I needed assistance or when I was committing a felony on a chocolate éclair. No one shouted at me; no one accused me of being stupid. Instead their help was at the ready, and they were quick to appreciate any improvements I made. These bakers gave me important lessons not only by providing critical feedback but also by showing that even a novice could be given a challenging task and helped to grow with assistance on the side. In other words, I didn't have to spend my two-week apprenticeship shaping croissants.

Many people of my age learned a great deal about cooking from watching Julia Child's PBS television programs. She was a master chef who became masterful through her own training at the Cordon Bleu school in France and the application of what she learned in her own kitchen. What she hoped to do was to introduce North Americans to the art of French cuisine—teaching them that any "ordinary" person in a home kitchen could produce a meal that was, at least, the equivalent of what a French chef did.

Julia taught us to be unafraid to tackle even what seemed to be the most difficult jobs, like boning a duck or producing a perfect *boeuf bourguignon*. She also taught us that when you dropped a chicken on the floor or when the layer of a cake broke into several pieces, all was not lost. In other words, "don't panic." The chicken could be wiped clean, cooked, and served, and no one at the dinner table would be the wiser. The broken pieces of the cake layer could be re-formed with a coat of chocolate icing, and no one would notice that either. Julia taught us to confront our fears, venture into the unknown, and make the most of our mistakes.

Learning about masterful teaching doesn't have to come from first-hand experience; some of it is learned from reading about such teachers.

Samuel Freedman's book *Small Victories* (1990) details a year in the life of Jessica Siegel, who taught Grade 12 at Seward Park High School on the Lower East Side of Manhattan, a neighborhood of low-income families, many of them recently arrived immigrants. The neighborhood was described as "having staggering social problems, and violent drug ridden streets that the students called home." The school had been ranked among the worst 10 percent of high schools in New York State.

Freedman sat in on Siegel's classes throughout the year, watching this master teacher at work. His book describes his observations from inside the classroom, relating what Siegel did that made not only a significant difference in the lives of her students but also how she enabled them to see better lives for themselves, aiding and abetting their applications for college and university entrance.

Teaching English to students with low expectations for themselves, and raising their hopes and their wishes for better lives, Siegel did more than just teach them about Walt Whitman, The Great Gatsby, and Martin Luther King, Jr. She broadened their horizons by, among other field trips, taking them to colleges, where they could meet with other students and learn about what was possible for them by way of further studies.

In Freedman's Afterword, he cites where some of her students were enrolled after Grade 12: University of Vermont, State University of New York at New Paltz, State University of New York at Binghamton, Manhattan Community College, Fashion Institute of Technology, Brooklyn College, Howard University, Hunter College, and LaGuardia Community College.

Freedman also notes that at Seward Park, spurred on by Siegel's work, the staff continues to "defy all expectations by sending 90% of each graduating class on to further education, carrying with them more than $100,000 worth of scholarships and grants."

Siegel, who gave more than 100 percent of her time, her expertise, her caring, her skills to her classes, understandably burned out and left Seward Park. One important lesson learned from reading about Jessica Siegel is how necessary it is for teachers to look after themselves, as they give their all to their students.

Another exemplar of a master teacher, who defied all odds and lifted his students from their low expectations of themselves to see them pass the Advanced Placement tests in Calculus and go on to graduate studies, was Jaime Escalante, about whom much has been written in newspapers and magazines, as well as documented in the film *Stand and Deliver*.

Escalante resigned from his office job as a computer specialist and applied for a position as math teacher at Garfield High School, in East Los Angeles, a neighborhood of low-income, Latin American families, many new immigrants, some undocumented. Many of the parents of the students spoke little or no English and had never finished school themselves. The neighborhood was rife with drugs, gangs, and other obstacles to a healthful life.

What Escalante did, besides his innovative approach to teaching math, was to teach his students to see themselves as capable, who could aspire to more than their neighborhood allowed. He called it "ganas"—the building of a desire to do better for themselves. He inspired them to excel regardless of their poor preparation in the lower school, difficult home situations, inadequate study habits, and all the incentives to fail that were endemic in their neighborhood.

Escalante's work with his students resulted in their becoming an elite group of top math students, opening the door for them to prestigious colleges and earning them college credits. His work took his students from their impoverished school preparations, barely able to add and subtract, to geometry, algebra, trigonometry, and mathematical analysis to AP calculus.

The work at the onset was brutal, and there were few successes. But after nine years, 127 of Escalante's students took the AP calculus test, and 85 passed—more than those at the prestigious Beverly Hills High. Escalante and his team shepherded hundreds of students through calculus and other higher math courses at Garfield in numbers unequalled before or since. Many of them made it to the best colleges in America and went onto high-profile careers in teaching science and engineering (Barham & Thomas, 2019).

What is clear from these accounts and others documenting what masterful teachers do is that they do much more than "give lessons." Through their teaching, they enable the students; they take their students to the next steps and open doors for them that they are able to use throughout their lives. These masterful teachers make a difference. What they do is additive in the most positive sense of the word.

If you have had one or more in your life, you are truly blessed, for you know what it is like to be Taught—with a capital "T."

Taking apart, piece by piece, what it is that makes a master teacher is the onus of this book. Through understanding the pieces, weaving them together into the whole called "teaching," and applying them in classroom practice lie the steps toward mastery.

Acknowledgments

This book could not have been written without the help of many people, and I want to acknowledge them with grateful appreciation for their support and their valuable input. First and foremost, to my beloved grandson, the wizard of Parksville, Simon, who is always available to bail me out of whatever computer problem that baffles me. My adorable great granddaughter, Maya, made a substantial contribution about her work in her Grade 4 IT class; her responses to my questions made clear the extent and nature of how IT is being used to enrich her curriculum.

Richard Dancy, the reference archivist at Simon Fraser University, is able to put his hands on previously published Wassermania now lodged in the archives, replying ever rapidly to my requests. Kelli Vogstead provided me with that five-year-old philosopher Eli's advice to new teachers, and I thank her for that terrific piece of work. Former colleague and friend Wally Eggert, coauthor of the *Profiles of Teaching Competency*, consented to allow me to include the Profiles in the Appendix of this text. In his book *What's Your Pronoun*, Dennis Baron gave me implicit permission to use "they" in lieu of the more awkward "he and she" as a pronoun for a singular noun—although it is still hard for me to do that.

Anne Bauer, editor for *Childhood Education*, has been generous in allowing me to adapt material from previously published articles in the journal, specifically "Changing Course: Rethinking Teacher Education Course Design" from *CE*, Vol. 93, 2017 and "Empowering Students Through Teacher Student Interactions: Teacher Talk That Makes a Difference," from *Focus on Later Childhood/Early Adolescence*, Winter, 1999, Vol. 2.

Thanks, too, to Sage Publishing, for permission to adapt material from "Leaving," published in the *Kappan*, June 2002, and to Teachers College

Press, for their permission to adapt material from previously published books, as cited in the relevant sections of the book.

And finally, to my reviewers, who took time from their busy schedules to read and give me feedback that enriched my thinking and my prose: Gary Squire, Tom O'Shea, Wally Eggert Bill Cliett, and Maureen McAllister—heartfelt thanks for your help and support.

Introduction

A common perception about teaching is of a teacher standing in front of a class of students, who remain quiet, listening to him or her teach the lessons that the students are required to learn. In fact, that perception is so ingrained in the minds of many that it has become the *idee fixe* of what teaching is all about. It is so deeply embedded that when the supervisor of instruction came to "observe" a first-year teacher and found her moving around the classroom, interacting individually with each student on a curriculum task she had given them, offering help, asking questions, giving support, and suggesting strategies, the supervisor sat for a few minutes, and then told her, "I'll come back when you're teaching."

The truth is that the complexity of what teachers do is incomprehensible to anyone who has not lived the experience. In fact, if one examines, in detail, the multidimensional, multilayered, multifaceted acts that a teacher performs each teaching day, it almost defies belief, for it is beyond heroic. Done well, it has a lasting impact on the students, influencing them for all the days of their lives. Done well, it leaves students altered for the better. Done well, it makes a positive difference in students' lives. It takes a trained observer to perceive and comprehend the various acts, both overt and subtle, that a teacher carries out during the course of a school day.

This is the onus of this book—to make explicit the professional tasks of a teacher in today's fast-changing world, where technology is rapidly replacing human interactions, where disinformation is daily fed to a gullible public, where funding and professional resources for schools are never enough, where students come to school carrying physical and emotional burdens that would daunt most adults, where the tasks of teachers are more demanding and more heartbreaking than ever before. How a teacher gives his or her all, and yet, manages to keep at the job, without burning out is a significant feature of the text.

Not only are these professional tasks identified and explained but suggestions are offered for how new and practicing teachers may further hone those skills that each task demands. In other words, "knowing" about the tasks is not enough; learning to apply them successfully is the key to becoming that master teacher.

The book begins with a preface and an introduction and is organized in eleven chapters. It provides a view of life in classrooms in chapter 1 and discusses the shocking realization of new teachers that the job of teaching is much more than they were prepared for in their preparatory programs in chapter 2. These initial parts of the book set the stage for the "meat and potatoes" of what follows.

The main chapters tackle some of the most important tasks that teachers do to ensure the quality of learning for each student.

These include coming to a fuller awareness of one's teaching goals and ensuring that teaching methods are congruent with those goals; ensuring that every teacher finds the ways and means to protect himself or herself from the burnout that master teaching demands; dealing successfully with the various and complex learning profiles of different students; using appropriate teacher-student interactions in classroom discussions; using appropriate curriculum materials that are compatible with subject and content goals, including making best use of technology as an adjunct to written materials; elevating teaching for thinking across the curriculum as a primary educational goal; and using evaluation strategies that enable the learner's progress.

Chapters 11 and 12 offer suggestions on how teachers can remain true to their beliefs and teaching goals within administrative constraints and, because every teacher needs to feel success, how they can identify those signs that his or her teaching has done some good. Some anecdotes are included that show "what's in it for teachers" who remain faithful to their beliefs and carry on doing herculean tasks every teaching day.

In the Conclusion, this teacher reflects on her teaching life—and what has made it worthwhile. A full copy of the Profiles of Teaching Competence is found in the Appendix.

For those who look to teaching from within and without the classroom, it is hoped that those readers will come to appreciate better the reality of what teachers do as they strive to make a difference in the lives of their students.

Chapter 1

Scenes from a Classroom

It's been one of those mornings when things never go right. The drive to school was hair-raising—roads slicked over with last night's freezing rain and a new snowfall, and yes, I skidded twice, nearly landing in a ditch. By the time I arrived at school, I was a wreck. Not the best way to greet twenty-seven Grade 6 students, who were energized by seeing their first snowfall of the season.

Coming into the class, I already felt exhausted. Before I even had time to shed my coat, Elisha was bombarding me with complaints about what had happened in the school yard. The rest of the group was restless, on a high. Was it the snow or the coming holiday season? Or something else? Often it's hard to know what causes kids to act up—something in the ethers? But there it was.

I was already wiped out from the drive and from working past midnight to read and give feedback on the students' papers. But I needed to gather my resources and face the day.

My classroom, as normal, is a whirlwind of activity both productive and aimless. Energy unleashed, as only can be found in a spirited group of active, healthy eleven-year-olds.

Matthew comes up to me, surrounded by three of his classmates, all talking at once. Someone took Matthew's book and he thinks it was Bernard. Bernard shouts that it was not him but that he thinks it was someone from another class. Everyone's talking at the same time, giving their views of what happened. I sit there trying to decide what to do, what to say, how to respond. Suddenly I feel too tired to cope. And there's the day's work to begin: the planning, the class meetings, the individual conferences, the setting up of the project groups. I try to get my mind focused in all the hubbub and remember to breathe out. Sigh.

I tell Matthew that I am unable to tell him what to do because I don't have enough data to make a good decision. He will have to figure it out for himself in a way that is fair to him and to Bernard. But when he does, I tell him to come and tell me what he has decided.

It is at times like these that I feel uncertain about what to do, always hoping that if I turn the problem back to the kids, they will find a way to figure it out.

I gather myself together and ask the class to settle down and get ready for the day. I ask Felicia and Kai to put away their tablets, and I see them grudgingly replace them in their backpacks. I ask the class to take out their planning books and to think about what each of them needs to include that morning, since we have been working on individualized programs in reading, math, and language arts, and to leave the afternoon open for beginning a new project in science.

Behind the scenes, I have worked at home to organize these science project plans, so that we will be addressing important concepts in the Grade 6 science curriculum. How it plays out in practice will tell me more about how their chosen groups will work together, which children show leadership in their groups and which are the followers, how they begin to organize their activities, and how they decide to obtain the information they need to complete their project work.

There is more learning for me in observing their behavior; yet, there is more that I need to know about how best to take them to the next steps in their learning.

By 9:30, most of them have completed their plans for the morning. I keep an eye peeled on Curtis, to see if he has been successful or if he is still doodling on the side of his plan book. No! A miracle! His plan is done and he gets out his book and begins to read. I write on the whiteboard "Reading Conferences" and ask if anyone wants to come up to read with me that morning. Several children rush to the board and scramble around to get their names listed. Six of them want conferences.

I retreat to my desk at the back of the room and get out my Reading Records for each child coming up for a conference. Before I get the records out, Jaime is already sitting next to me, with his book, waiting.

He is recently arrived, and his English is "emerging." But he is sweet, tries very hard, and wants very much to be a part of this new life, of this classroom, of this community. I need to listen to his reading carefully, understand what his immediate needs are, and help him gain the word analysis tools to become more successful. This I must do, without harming his ego; I cannot use the skill development exercises that are written for primary grades. I need to design some more sophisticated phonic and world analysis activities for him. More work tonight.

Although there is a hum in the classroom, the children are engaged and on task, and the background hum sounds to me as if it is productive, rather than aimless. I finish the reading conferences, make notes on each child's Reading Record, and move on to work in math. Several children are presenting similar difficulty with fractions, and I ask them to come to work with me in a group. I have prepared a skill exercise that should engage them and give me an idea of who is grasping the concepts and who needs further help. Every response a child makes tells me about their competence, their difficulties, their skill development. I try to remember all of this, so that I can record it on their individual record sheets that I keep, to give me firsthand information about their individual learning needs and to decide on what I need to do next for each of them.

Before I realize it, the recess bell sounds, and the kids leave their books and gather at the door. The new snow on the ground doesn't daunt them; they will enjoy it but will likely return to the room wet and cold.

I work my way down to the staff room and grab my mug. There's just enough time for a quick cup of tea. But before I put my tea bag into the mug, the phone rings and I'm called down to the office. Curtis's mother wants to know why he is not bringing any of his assignments home.

THE TEACHER AS DECISION MAKER

The life of a teacher is one of making a constant litany of decisions—one of the most demanding aspects of a teacher's work. Teachers are responsible for choosing curriculum experiences that address not only the curriculum requirements of the grade but also individual learning needs. Often this demands creating new materials, since what is available may not be appropriate. As is seen in the vignette above, teachers choose the ways in which they deal with the emotional, social, and intellectual needs of the students as well as giving each the attention they need so that improved learning may result.

Teachers make choices about evaluating students' written and oral work, making diagnoses of performance on specific tasks, making thoughtful judgments about the whole of a student's performance over an interval of time, and choosing how to report all of this in comprehensible ways to anxious parents.

Teachers choose if and when and how to work with individuals, small groups, and the whole class, even though the approach to each may require different sets of skills and different types of teacher-student interactions. They must be masters of the interactive process, choosing when to ask questions, which kinds of questions to ask, when to inform, when to show how, when to clarify students' ideas, when to challenge their thinking, and when not to respond at all.

A teacher chooses how to respond to students' behavior problems, choosing when and how to be tough and firm without diminishing a student's dignity, and when to overlook the indiscretion. A teacher chooses how to organize the classroom for instruction and must be flexible enough to make shifts in that organization plan so that the learning goals and organizational scheme are congruent.

The teacher must be the composer, the orchestrator, and the conductor of the classroom symphony, if the players are to make beautiful music. On top of all of that, teachers make choices about attending professional development activities, reading what is current, participating in meetings and workshops, and making intelligent decisions about what new ideas are of real value and which lack true educational merit.

If this list sounds extensive and exhaustive, it barely scratches the surface. Teachers make hundreds of decisions each day, from the trivial to the very complex. It is no secret that the professional functioning of teachers is riddled with decision-making that would tax a Solomon.

If that is not enough, the decisions that teachers make are rarely clear-cut. They involve considerable judgment, knowledge, skill, and intuition, as well as thoughtful consideration of data. Often the wisdom of a judgment is revealed only after time, and not seen at first. That is why teachers need to place trust in their judgments until the results can be seen.

Such decision-making is not only complex, it is often full of tension, ambiguity, and risk. And to make matters worse, decisions are more than often made alone, without the consulting help of another professional.

There is, of course, no value-free choice. To accept that principle is the starting point from which teachers ease themselves into increased awareness that each choice represents a tilting toward some value position. Knowing that many choices, if not most, are encumbered by "outside baggage" and that choices come with inevitable consequences guides us in the process of choosing.

Even in schools where teachers' decision-making prerogatives are sacrosanct, they do not have unlimited choices. Regardless of whether freedom of choice abounds or is to some degree restricted, decision-making is facilitated when teachers know what they are choosing, are clear about the options, are aware of the pressures (personal, administrative, parental, political, educational) that bear on the choice, are aware of their beliefs that tilt them in the direction of a decision, and have an idea of the potential consequences of the decision. All of these conditions do not encumber choosing but instead facilitate the action of deciding.

When teachers are clear about all these things, it is easier for them to choose.

And this, too, is teaching.

Chapter 2

Beginnings

Some Advice for New Teachers

It's his very first day on the job. He has been newly hired to replace a teacher who has had, suddenly, to go off on maternity leave. On the one hand, he comes into the class when the organization, the schedules, the program, and the management systems are in place. On the other hand, he will have to establish rapport with a class deeply disappointed to see their teacher leave them.

His preparation in student teaching was in an intermediate grade; he is not only a beginning teacher but a beginner to a primary classroom. He is unsure about seven-year-olds, but good sense tells him that they are likely to need more instruction, more help, more guidance, more direction than those eleven-year-olds in his student teaching classroom.

He tries to draw on some of the lessons he learned in his course work—subjects required for an education degree. But despite a respectable grade point average, he is uncertain about how to proceed and unclear about curriculum, about individual learning styles, about behavior problems, about classroom management, about everything. Suddenly all of what he thought he knew about how to teach becomes a sea of uncertainty, the children strangers in a strange land, the procedures alien, the task before him like a giant maze, in which he needs to find his way.

The children respond to his uncertainty by showing their own insecurities. What seemed like an orderly group becomes more and more excited, unnerved, anxious; the buzz builds to a clamor and suddenly erupts in what seems to him like chaos. He finds himself shouting, calling for order, asking the children, whose names he has yet to learn, to sit down and be quiet. Ten minutes into the day's program and already things are out of control.

To add insult to injury, Greg admonishes him: Mrs. Kramer never did it that way.

Harry Summers is not the only teacher who has faced his first teaching assignment with a sense of being overwhelmed by the job. Studies of the transition between preservice preparations and the in-service demands of the job indicate that such feelings are common. Among them, managing behavior, the diverse needs of students, time constraints, work overload, and conflicts with parents and other professionals appear to be the largest issues of tension for beginning teachers (Meister & Jenks, 2012).

Given those data, the likelihood is great that when new teachers begin to "fly solo," experiencing a great flood of uncertainty and anxiety, they are more than likely to fall back on what they know best: their own in-school experiences as students. For after all, sitting in elementary and secondary classrooms for more than a dozen years, totaling about 15,000 hours of immersion in the culture of schooling, this has to trump the mere 36 hours of preservice preparation coursework. Perhaps that is one way to explain why teaching practices are so immune to change; the institutional press of a new teacher's own elementary and secondary school experiences is so powerful an education that it informs current practice. New teachers, full of uncertainty, cling to what they know best.

WHAT'S WRONG WITH TEACHER EDUCATION?

He stands at the front of the room, with the authority of his several graduate degrees behind him, as the students sit and listen to him describe what constitutes "good teaching." He admonishes them to be mindful of individual learning differences, of classroom management, of children who present learning problems. They are to be knowledgeable about curriculum requirements issued by school and state boards of education, to understand how to maintain classroom control and how to deal with behavior problems.

The list of "shoulds" is formidable, and the students copy them dutifully into their notebooks or laptops, ready to recall them for the final exam. This course is one of the requirements for an education degree that would qualify them to become certified. To bring about more hands-on student involvement, students are given assignments generating lesson plans in the abstract, without any consideration of the make-up of an actual class, and research projects that have as little to do with classroom life as chalk to cheese.

In the thirty-six hours of required coursework, not a single course deviates from this teaching model: teacher-centered lectures, and a long list of "to-dos" that are supposed to prepare preservice students to face their own students not only with competence but with panache. What is noticeably absent from these programs is the enabling of students to connect theory to the realities of classroom life, so that when preservice students face their own classrooms, they would have, at the very least, some fundamental teaching skills at their fingertips and the competence to use them effectively.

Little wonder that upon facing that first class of a highly energetic bunch of third graders, he fumbled and stumbled and mumbled his way through the day, barely able to recall the many "shoulds" and unhappily unable to find the means to put them into practice, giving voice once again to the most frequently cited criticism of teacher education: the yawing abyss between "telling" preservice students in education classes how they should teach and providing them with meaningful opportunities to translate the "shoulds" to classroom applications (Wassermann, 2017).

Authors Zeichner (2018) and Levine (2006) have studied teacher education programs and both have written about the inadequacies of teacher preparation. "By almost any standard, many, if not most, of the nation's 1,450 schools, colleges and departments of education are doing a mediocre job of preparing teachers" (Zeichner, 2018).

Levine's (2006) comprehensive study of graduates of teacher education programs reported that despite a few "model" teacher education programs, the majority of teachers are prepared in programs that have low admission and graduation standards, "clinging to an outdated, historically flawed vision of teacher education, resulting in many graduating without the skills and knowledge they need to become effective teachers."

There are many reasons for this, reasons that make such programs resistant to change. In many colleges and universities, education is one of the "cash cows" of the institution, with low admission standards that make it possible for their large enrollments to support financially those other programs that are in budgetary shortfall. Many professors who come to teach in these programs are themselves without experience as teachers in the public schools and are more obsessed with their own tenure and promotion aspects than they are about the practice of teaching. Very few have a clear idea of how to design a course that emphasizes how to connect the ideas they are promoting with the realities of classroom life.

Required courses are a hodgepodge of what professors want to teach, rather than what would constitute the acquisition and development of effective teaching skills for new teachers. Curriculums are not coherent; they do not enable students to master the skills and knowledge needed by teachers at specific kinds of schools and with specific kinds of learners. There is a huge disconnect between theory and practice.

Of course, this is not true of all teacher education programs—but unhappily true of too many. And given that teacher education programs are not likely to change any time soon, despite the overwhelming evidence about their failings, what are beginning teachers to do as they face those terrifying first days, weeks, months of their own classroom practice?

Chapter 2

SOME ADVICE FOR "NOO TEECHRS"

Eli, a five-year-old in a kindergarten class, was asked for his advice for new teachers. In his emerging writing style, he offered the following suggestions:

4 imprtint Things for Noo Teechrs to Member
1. *Sumtims ther are no rite ansers*
2. *Its eezier with a buddy*
3. *Alwees smile*
4. *Whan yor braen gets hevy be sher to empte sum and thn play and get sum rest.*[1]

Five-year-olds have a wonderful capacity to understand what it takes for new teachers to get through that difficult and highly challenging first year of teaching, without an overriding sense of failure, without an eye to pack it all in and look for a job slinging hamburgers at McDonalds.

Adding to Eli's advice, the following is offered, humbly, from one who has faced the dragon and lived to tell the tale.

First, a reminder from Hippocrates: Do no harm. Your students should feel better, more capable at the end of a school day than they did at the beginning. If they feel worse, less able, then their school day has hurt them rather than helped them. No matter what you do, no matter how you bungle, how ineptly you carry out your lesson plans, first, do no harm.

Second, be clear about your teaching goals for your class. Never mind what the curriculum guides say; never mind those noble and high-minded objectives. What is it that you hope to accomplish? What, if you had a magic wand, positive changes would you wish to see in your students at the end of this teaching year. Of course, it helps to be realistic about them! Aiming for the moon may result in frustration and defeat before you get started.

It may be a good idea to start with these principles—these goal statements that you would aspire to in the quality and quantity of what you teach. And write them down in a clear and realistic way, eschewing the jargon. Do you want them to become more enabled? Empowered? Thoughtful? Independent thinkers? Do you want to inspire in them a love of learning? Do you want them to be kinder and more compassionate with each other? Respectful of each other's ideas and persons?

For as sure as snow is followed by little boys with sleds, your clearly stated and clearly understood teaching goals will guide the how and what you do. Your goals will inform your teaching strategies and curriculum choices.

And it is not simplistic to ask yourself at the end of each teaching day how what you did served to help your students take a step further in realizing those goals.

Third, find a teacher whom you admire, whom is doing with his or her class what you hope and expect to do yourself, and make a concerted effort to study that teacher both by observation and through discussion. You will find that such experienced and highly professional teachers are happy to help a "newbie," and they will give you not only advice but many suggestions for what you can do to help you realize your teaching goals. Study that teacher as if there is no tomorrow, as if your teaching life depended on it!

Fourth, find ways to keep yourself mentally and physically healthy. Eli suggests that "when your brain gets heavy, empty some, play and get some rest." Teaching, which is an all-consuming profession, should not be allowed to consume you to the extent that you lose perspective and become exhausted. Play is a wonderful antidote for replenishing one's resources. Insure that you include "mental health" times in your working week.

And last, but hardly least, is the reminder that learning to teach is a lifelong process. There are no miracles, no magic bullets that will turn a new teacher to Super Teacher. Learning from mistakes, from egregious errors, is what teaches us what we could be doing instead. Beating oneself up from errors of judgment and of strategy is a quick road to burnout. Another five-year-old's advice on that score is "Give yourself a break."

LAST WORDS

The profession of teaching is not for everyone. Those who choose it and who remain in the job, giving their all, and truly making a difference in the lives of their students, are clear: this is where they want to be. This is what they want to be doing. So as some last words to new teachers, the final admonition is for any new teacher to be sure, absolutely sure, that this is what you want to do: that working with students is what you enjoy and what gives you satisfaction.

If you are not getting that joy, that satisfaction, then find something different. Life is too short to stay in a job that is ultimately too stressful or too unsatisfying, no matter how secure tenure is. The stress and the lack of satisfaction is defeating, and it will leak out onto the students.

The counterpart of that is, enjoy your students. If you are not finding pleasure in being with them, it's time to consider another career.

NOTE

1. Courtesy of Kelli Vogstad, principal, Surrey Public Schools, British Columbia.

Chapter 3

The Professional Tasks of the Teacher

Faculty associates at Simon Fraser University play a key role in the preparation of students in the teacher education program. They are recruited from their classroom teaching positions for a two-year appointment to the Faculty of Education. The theory behind these secondments is that education students might benefit more from learning from those with recent firsthand classroom experiences.

Taken from the field and parachuted into the Faculty of Education, with a two-week orientation, faculty associates are assigned groups of fifteen students who have been placed in student teaching assignments. Their job is to visit these classrooms, observe the student teacher in action, liaise with the sponsor teacher, and set up postobservation conferences with the student teacher to evaluate, advise, consult, and make recommendations for the improvement of practice.

What does the faculty associate look for? What kinds of teaching operations are observable, explicit, and essential to a healthful, thriving, educationally sound teaching environment? What is good teaching?

Good classroom discipline?
Covering the curriculum?
Willing to learn?
Good rapport with the students?
Enthusiasm for teaching?
Professional attitude?
Neat bulletin boards?

THE DEVELOPMENT OF AN ASSESSMENT INSTRUMENT TO EVALUATE TEACHING COMPETENCE

Wassermann and Eggert (1976) initiated a field research to try to identify those teaching behaviors that experienced teachers considered to be significant "tells" of teaching excellence. The assessment tool would, when completed, be used to evaluate student teaching competence with an eye toward professional development, rather than to produce a grade.

They began by surveying a large group of practicing teachers, asking them to define what they considered to be some essential characteristics of what good teachers do. Their primary objective was to use professional teachers' responses to create a "competency instrument" that would be used to assess student teaching performance and enable professional growth toward those standards.

The teachers were advised to focus their responses on four criteria that would illuminate their ideas of competence. For example:

1. The competence must reflect the observable work of the teacher in the classroom. (In other words, in examining a surgeon's competency to do a kidney transplant, we would expect that whether they had the skills would be pretty much determined by that doctor's performance on the operating table. Whether they had read at least two books on kidney transplants would be a meaningless measure, unless they demonstrated the ability to translate what had been read into surgical practice.)
2. While the competence should focus on behavior that is observable, it should not dwell on the more insignificant behavioral characteristics, just because they are the ones that are most easily seen.
3. The competence should relate clearly to the furtherance of student learning.
4. The competence should reflect the educational values to which we, as professionals, aspire (Wassermann & Eggert, 1976).

PROFILES OF TEACHING COMPETENCY

More than 100 "competencies" were gathered from the teachers' survey, and the next step in the process was to organize them into related categories. Selecting observable behaviors from this large group of items was, at the very first, a matter of determining what was important in teaching practice. Obviously, it was not possible to have an instrument that included everything. There were many alternatives to be considered and decisions made about what to include. Guiding those choices was the overarching criterion: Is this what we really value in teaching?

Once a preliminary list was created, each item was considered in relationship to student learning. To be able to say, "If the teacher does this competently, student learning will be enhanced" became the second step in deciding whether that item of teaching behavior would be included. Once the list had been winnowed down, it was submitted to professional colleagues who had experience working with and assessing student teachers. Their feedback was used to further refine the list of competencies.

Next, an examination of the literature in teacher education that dealt with evaluation of teaching led to further refinements.

As the list of competencies continued to be refined, they appeared to fall into three categories. One group was related to the idea of "teacher as a role model." Another group was related to the ways in which teachers interacted with their students, as these behaviors were seen to create the conditions that facilitate students' learning. The third category in which the remaining items seemed to fall related to the triangular relationship between the teacher, the students, and the curriculum.

In the final culling, nineteen items of teaching competency were described in behavioral profiles, and each was paired with a negative view of the same behavior. In that way, it was made explicit that some teacher behaviors were facilitative of student learning, while others were considered detrimental to learning. Later revisions of the Profiles added a twentieth profile.

Field testing of the Profiles of Teaching Competency (Wassermann & Eggert, 1973, 1986, 1988, 1994) was done with a sample of 100 student teachers. In this field test, student teachers rated themselves on the instrument, along with ratings by their sponsor teachers and faculty associates. Interviews with students, sponsor teachers, and faculty associates were conducted to obtain feedback. The items that produced a high level of discrepancy among the raters pointed to more work needed in refining the Profiles.

The Profiles of Teaching Competency that resulted from this research then began its long-term use as an evaluative instrument to assess the teaching performance of preservice teachers in the Faculty of Education at Simon Fraser University.

CATEGORIES OF TEACHING COMPETENCY

The twenty behavioral profiles seen as related to competent teaching performance do not include everything that a good teacher does. They do represent one perspective of what are considered to be some of the more important teaching functions that contribute to student learning—in other words, what master teachers do.

The profiles are grouped into three categories:

The Teacher as Person. The nine profiles in this group reflect important and observable characteristics of the person in charge of the classroom. Since the classroom climate depends, to a large extent, on the teacher's temperament, intellectual openness, respect for the students, warmth, and enthusiasm for teaching, this category stands first among the three.

The Teacher and the Kids: Interactions. The six profiles in this group reflect the many ways in which teachers interact with their students, including their ability to observe, diagnose, and deal with behaviors that impede learning; their use of higher-order questions to promote student thinking; and the authenticity of their responses.

The Teacher, the Kids, and the "Stuff"—Classroom Life. The five profiles in this group represent the ways in which teachers, students, and curriculum are interwoven into the warp and woof of a rich classroom environment.

The Profiles of Teaching Competency form the template of what follows in the succeeding chapters—those essential acts of teaching that are significant to a productive and rich classroom life. In each chapter, as well, suggestions are also made as to how teachers may take the steps needed to progress toward greater mastery in teaching.

A copy of the Profiles of Teaching Competency is found in the Appendix. Permission is granted by the author to duplicate the Profiles for use with student teachers.

Chapter 4

Teacher as Person

A good teacher must have patients [sic] with the students and parents, [at conferences] when they don't understand something. They must have good humor and laugh when something is funny, but they have to be strict sometimes. They must always have confidence in the students, show them and lead them on the right road to sucess [sic]. They should be able to hold their temper and treat the student in a nice way. Not only do they teach them from the book but in ways of making it fun to do it. They must know what work a child needs; otherwise it makes it bad for him or her. They must always have love even for the bad ones. (Robert Meagher, Grade 6, Lee Road School)

Not everyone is cut out to be a teacher. Some have a natural gift for the work and their training serves to further their abilities and talents. Some come to professional education by default. The expectation is that as they learn more from their preservice experiences, they will become more certain that teaching is for them. Others are soon disabused of the notion that they actually want to spend their lives working in classrooms. This is an important awareness for no one wants to spend a lifetime in a job for which they are emotionally and mentally unsuited.

But having chosen teaching, with a clear and unbiased view of what the job demands, having a true and realistic notion of what it means to devote one's life to the learning of others, what can be said about how a teacher continues to learn and grow on the job, making a difference to the lives of others, without burning out?

If the "teacher is the key" to what happens in a classroom, what are some essential components that contribute to success? What are the important ingredients that allow teachers to not only survive but flourish? And how can teachers protect themselves from the exhaustion that comes from, arguably, one of the most demanding and emotionally consuming jobs of all the professions?

GROWING TEACHERS

It is a given that a classroom is a multilayered, multifaceted fabric of experiences that, to the untrained observer, must seem like a crazy quilt, with so much happening at the same time that it is impossible to take it all in. Considering that this is what good classrooms are like, rich with enough human drama for a hundred years of soap opera, it's no wonder that teachers are constantly searching to find solutions to the various and far-reaching problems that they face each teaching day. Answers, after all, reduce the tension and restore a sense of security, the feeling that one has it all under control.

Deciding what to do, choosing from many possible courses of action, is a high-risk endeavor, full of potential hazards. This is the stuff that keeps teachers awake at nights. And when they finally fall asleep, it makes for disturbing dreams.

What advice, then, can be given to teachers that would enable them to face these classroom complexities, not only to make it through each teaching day but with enough left over to face tomorrow? To live with the realization that many problems have no clear "fixes," that some defy solutions, and that sometimes the best course of action is no action?

BEING CLEAR ABOUT WHAT'S IMPORTANT

One of the most demanding task of classroom teachers, the one that requires the most searching, evaluating, and examining, and the one that underlies most of what a teacher does, is that of decision-making. In the face of many alternatives, teachers must decide what it is they are going to do, what they are going to say, how they are going to say it, and whether they are going to react or remain neutral. In the presence of numerous options, teachers make choices that prescribe what they do.

Teachers' decisions about what to do and how to do it are influenced by many factors: their earlier educational experiences, their reading, their discussions with colleagues, community pressure, parental interests, and, of course, the dictates of administrative fiats. In this maze, the teacher continually evaluates and decides. Underlying those decisions are the values that the teacher holds dear. In other words, action is dictated by what the teacher considers important. For despite those external pressures, the strong motivation to choose comes from what the teacher believes is right and good.

A teacher's fundamental beliefs about the many and varied acts that constitute teaching practice are seeded and grown from their own classroom experiences as students, from their preservice professional training, from their reading, from their interactions with their teachers and colleagues, and from current events. When the teacher's beliefs are clear, they form the basis for how a teacher chooses and how a teacher acts.

When beliefs are unclear, they may result in teaching practices that are uneven, inconsistent, and perhaps even dysfunctional. What's more, a teacher who espouses a certain belief and whose classroom practices are at variance with that belief comes across as evasive, defensive, and inconsistent.

Being clear about one's own beliefs and values is the bedrock of what a teacher does, how a teacher chooses, and what a teacher decides is important. Recognizing "what's important" is the largest influence on the shaping of those beliefs.

There is no clear course of action that would aid and abet such clarity, but a few suggestions may be helpful.

- Reading in the literature of education, psychology, sociology, history—especially those books that have been written by authors one respects, whose positions about schooling and youth and the culture are highly regarded and make sense to you.
- Discussions with experienced teachers whose classroom work you admire and respect.
- Visiting classrooms of teachers whose classroom work you admire and respect.
- Attending professional workshops and in-service professional days.
- Having many opportunities to discuss what you believe with others who may help to further clarify your thinking.
- Keeping abreast with what is current in the news, not only about education but about your community, your city, your state or province, your country, the world.
- Keeping an ongoing check to ascertain whether what you are doing is consonant with your expressed beliefs.

None of the above is a surefire guarantee that clarity of beliefs will emerge, but it is a strong beginning.

Chapter 4

SHARPENING YOUR PROBLEM-SOLVING SKILLS

There is, of course, an intimate relationship between problem-solving and decision-making. Problems are better solved when the choices of what to do are clearer. While problem-solving is dependent to a large degree on the choices one makes, making good choices does not necessarily lead to improved solutions.

Classrooms are hotbeds of problems that run the gamut from major, to those of lesser consequence. No matter how teachers may try to "smooth" the running of their classrooms, problems inevitably arise that are unexpected and that create glitches in any semblance of smooth functioning.

- *Bobby wet his pants and everyone is laughing at him.*
- *No one wants Annette in their group. She's a dork.*
- *My mother said we should not be using plastic bags anymore for our lunches.*
- *I think you should let us use our tablets to help us with our math assignments.*
- *Mr. Biot's class has more homework than we have. You aren't giving us enough homework. How are we going to be prepared for Grade 8?*
- *Using Facebook is a good way to make a lot of new friends.*
- *Why can't we use our cell phones during independent study time?*
- *I couldn't finish my homework. My mother is sick and I needed to help her.*
- *I don't want to sit next to her. She smells bad.*

What enables better solutions is a teacher's skill in identifying the problem at the very first step of the process. When the nature of the problem becomes clearer, the strategies for moving ahead become clearer as well.

An important aspect of improved problem-solving skills is the teacher's ability to assess, in the process, what is proceeding well and where any breakdown occurs, so that a change of strategy is required. Being stuck in a dysfunctional mode is counterproductive; being able to say, "hey, this isn't working," scrap the plan and create a new plan, or strategy, takes a lot of autonomy and confidence in self. But persevering with a dysfunctional plan is a no-brainer. Everybody loses.

To bring all of this down to a lower level of abstraction, here's an example of how this works in a classroom:

The sixth-grade teacher was concerned that some of her students were revealing negative and racist attitudes toward others, both inside and outside of the classroom. She saw the problem as one in which she needed to promote more socially conscious and respectful attitudes toward others and thought long and hard about how she might go about doing this. This, then, became the problem to be solved.

At the very first, she recognized that admonishing the students to behave more kindly and respectfully toward others was a nonstarter. They might do this in her presence, but such behaviors would very likely not endure outside of the classroom. How then to develop a program that emphasized respect and empathy for peoples of all races, colors, ethnic origins?

Her first approach was to present the problem boldly to the students, making them aware that this was a problem that they all faced, and seemed to her to be counterproductive to healthful classroom functioning. After presenting the problem to them, she elicited their responses and questions. At first, there was considerable denial that such a problem existed. The students did not want to "own" their negative behavior toward others.

The teacher's responses to the students was to listen, to reflect, and to raise questions and promote their further examination of the various ways in which she had perceived these situations occurring. She was careful not to put any student on the spot, not to fault, or to blame. In that way, she hoped the discussions would become more open, more revealing, more honest.

When, finally, the students were able to acknowledge that such a problem might exist, she then asked them for ideas about how they might go about becoming more respectful to each other. Since this was a huge undertaking for them, she began by asking them to form discussion groups to, first, give examples of how such behavior could be hurtful to others, where such ideas about others came from, and what would be some suggestions for changing those attitudes and behaviors.

She asked each group to take notes that would be shared in a whole class discussion on these three questions. Her belief was that when the students could become a part of the problem-solving experience, they would have greater ownership of the solutions they were proposing.

An important recognition in tackling classroom problems is the likelihood that the solution does not necessarily "disappear" the problem. There may be elements that remain, students who are not responsive, recurrence of what seemed, at first, to be dealt with. And when that occurs, it is easy to give in to feelings of frustration and defeat. That is when it is important to take the long view, recognizing that all is *not* lost, that even a small victory is a gain, that one never knows when seeds that have been planted give rise, in later days, months, years, to roses.

No, Virginia, there's no Santa Claus. But "teaching is like dropping ideas into the letter box of the human subconscious. You know when they are posted, but you never know when they will be received or in what form" (Christensen, in Gulette, 1982).

Chapter 4

THE IMPORTANCE OF BEING REAL

Your actions speak so loudly I can't hear what you are saying. (Old Aleut philosophy)

It is sometimes called authenticity, sometimes congruence, sometimes genuineness in referring to a person's ability to be himself or herself, to be "real" (Rogers, 1961; Leahy, 2009; Carkhuff, 1969; Moustakas, 1966; Greenberg & Johnson, 1978). It has been suggested that genuineness is the most important condition in effective human relationships, basic to all helping professions (Truax & Mitchell, 1971).

At the opposite end of that behavioral continuum is phoniness, or defensiveness, the donning of a "professional facade" to hide one's genuine self. Sidney Jourard (1964) called it "character armor"—that invisible, psychological shield one puts up as protection from feelings of vulnerability. Character armor serves to hide a person's real self, both from self and from others.

Sometimes this character armor is seen in nurses' or doctors' "bedside manner," who use it as a means of coping with repeated encounters with suffering, demanding patients. "If the armor is effective, it permits the practitioner to go about his/her duties unaffected by disturbing feelings of pity, anger, inadequacy, or insecurity" (Jourard, 1964).

There are parallels between bedside manner and the professional demeanor taken on by an insecure teacher. As character armor is seen in health practitioners, so is the "role" acted out by teachers who feel anxious and vulnerable; who feel the need to appear no less than perfect to students; who feel that they must communicate a persona of cool, detached, professionalism. The need to mask feelings of anxiety and insecurity, to appear flawlessly competent, is a strong force in maintaining that professional facade.

A teacher's character armor may serve as a defense against an overly critical supervisor, against unhappy and harassing parents, against encounters with hurt and hurting children, whose obvious suffering and demanding behaviors are too much for a sensitive teacher to endure, if he or she is going to maintain professional competence. It is most often seen in new teachers, who come into the classroom with strong feelings of anxiety that often accompany lack of experience.

When a teacher has to face the anxiety that accompanies the many challenges of the normal classroom, it is no wonder that he or she may try to escape further stress by assuming a detached professional manner.

There are, unfortunately, prices to pay. Next to parents, teachers are frequently the most significant others in the lives of students. And when a teacher comes across as acting a role, the students learn that the teacher is artificial and therefore cannot be trusted; that the teacher is putting on an act and therefore not genuine; and that there is an absence of openness and of true feeling.

That absence of genuineness has negative effects on teachers themselves. While teachers may trade off their feelings of vulnerability and mask their own insecurities behind a professional facade, they lose some of their own emotional well-being in the bargain. The result may be increased defensiveness and further alienation from self.

Being openly honest with oneself is probably one of the most difficult challenges to personal development. Everyone wants to think of himself or herself as genuine; no one wants to own up to playing a role. But defensiveness builds strong, nearly impermeable walls to genuineness.

Alas, there is no magic formula to break down those walls. One can press one's navel all day and still wind up with strong defenses that defy breaching. However, a search into the literature and research on professionals in helping roles suggest some courses of action that teachers might take to shed those counterproductive roles and move toward becoming more authentic (e.g., Gazda, 1973; Gordon, 1974; Rogers & Steven, 1967; Truax & Mitchell, 1971; Greenberg & Johnson, 1978).

Some researchers have suggested that training in active listening would aid teachers in becoming more open and truer to their own feelings (Greenberg & Johnson, 1978; Carkhuff, 1969). This notion about being true to one's feelings seems to be a strong factor in genuineness; the opposite would be to deny or hide feelings or to pretend otherwise than what was being felt.

In the current literature and research into the development of genuineness, several additional factors emerge. But to distill what professionals claim to improve genuineness are the following suggestions. It's helpful to remember that no one said this was easy.

1. Level the playing field. In your interactions with students (and with adults), if you have to assume that you are better, wiser, stronger, more knowledgeable, more powerful, then chances are that you will be holding on to a professional facade that keeps you from being yourself. If you can respond to others (students and adults) without guise or guile or artifice, then you have a better chance of being genuine.

2. Be respectful of all of those with whom you interact, including even those kids who drive you crazy. This is helped by trying to see yourself in the shoes of the "other." When you can do that, when you can be empathic with the needs, feelings, wishes, and hopes of others, you have a better chance of being genuine.

3. Put down your cell phone and watch and listen to what is happening all around you. Use that data to inform your further interactions with others.

4. Use language in your communications that is easily understood by others. If you hide behind obfuscations and retreat into arcane and incomprehensible

speech, you are isolating yourself from others, rather than connecting with them.

5. Real, genuine, human connections are made through open dialogue. One has to reveal oneself in the process of speaking truth, honestly and openly.

What is obviously true is that all of this is easier said than done. What is also true is that shedding the mantle of defensiveness and becoming more open, more genuine, more honest in one's interactions with students is not done in a day or a week. It's one of those processes that takes both a fuller awareness of oneself in human relationships and the willingness and motivation to keep working at becoming more authentic.

There are several important caveats that warrant consideration on a person's pathway to dropping the barriers behind which we hide our true selves. First, there are occasions when it is wiser, smarter, more sensible to remain nondisclosing. In other words, even highly genuine people do not necessarily open themselves to others all the time, without regard to whom, and to what the situation warrants. Sometimes, one chooses tact over disclosure; you don't tell your mother-in-law, when she asks, that her apple pie was underbaked and inedible. Not every situation is amenable to open dialogue.

Second, there are likely occasions when one's true feelings are left unspoken. Here again, a choice is made, not to be phony, but to be tactful when a situation demands more tact than openness.

Third, it is sometimes difficult to make oneself vulnerable, because personal situations, conditions of psychological safety, preclude such openness. Once again, the teacher chooses how to act, how to respond. It would be fair to say that when circumstances demand that self-protection, a choice is made that does not, in the long term, negate the overall genuine self.

None of the suggestions for becoming more genuine are guarantees to the gaining of insight into one's professional functioning, but it is hoped that they serve to raise awareness in gaining a bit more understanding about the ways in which one functions in real time and the behaviors that you believe might be counterproductive to the kind of teacher/person you hoped to be.

> *"Real isn't how you are made,"* said the Skin Horse. *"It's a thing that happens to you. When a child loves you for a long, long time, not just to play with, but REALLY loves you, then you become Real." "Does it hurt?"* asked the Rabbit. *"Sometimes,"* said the Skin Horse, for he was always truthful (Bianco, 1958).

DEVELOPING CONFIDENCE IN SELF

What happens in the real world of the school, where teachers are very much alone and the "institutional press" is pushing down hard to get teachers to conform to the status quo? How do teachers hold on to their beliefs and teach in the ways that are consistent with their beliefs about their students and what it takes to help them to grow and learn? How do teachers maintain their integrity and live to teach another day?

Perhaps the single, most important dimension of self that ensures survival is the teacher's self-confidence. Confidence, of course, comes from experience; the more one is successful at one's job, the more confidence grows. This makes the new teacher especially vulnerable, since that experience is either lacking or in short supply. So how do new teachers survive those first 100 teaching days as they gather the experience that builds their confidence?

Initial confidence comes from one's beliefs in oneself, that deep, overriding belief that one is "up to" the formidable tasks of classroom teaching. No one can give a teacher that kind of belief—not your mother, or your father, or your college professor. A person must discover it in oneself, pull it out from deep inside, and breathe life into it.

If one is confident, this will exude out of you from every pore, in the way you walk and talk; in the way you stand and sit; in the ways in which you interact with colleagues and administrators, parents and students. Your confidence in yourself will reassure them and they will have confidence in you. You will be perceived as confident only if your verbal and nonverbal behavior communicates your confidence. When you are confident, you also earn the respect of others.

Strengthening confidence in oneself is the key not only to a teacher's survival but to one's psychological and physical health, as well as to one's continued growth as a professional.

Some questions to consider in thinking about improving one's self-confidence:

1. In what ways does your "self-talk" contribute to/undermine your confidence in yourself?
2. What strategies can you use to build your self-confidence?
3. What strategies are unconsciously used to keep your self-confidence low?
4. Why is it difficult for you to express openly your positive talents?
5. What are the perceived consequences of making mistakes?
6. What needs to be "perfect" undermine your feelings of confidence?

Understanding the unconscious mental strategies that are in place to diminish confidence in self is a small way of beginning to appreciate what they are, how they function, and what can be done to alter that process. In addition, a few other suggestions may be helpful:

- Keeping a journal to record, especially, those impediments to building your confidence
- Creating new "self-talk" that recognizes and honors your successes
- Talking to a respected and trusted colleague about your feelings
- Doing something brave and new once a week and giving yourself a "reward" for what you have done
- Having open discussion with your students and asking them what they appreciate about what you are doing
- Ensuring that you take care of yourself physically and emotionally

TAKING CARE OF YOURSELF

Dedicated teachers are notoriously neglectful about their own physical health. When coming down with a cold and feeling rotten, they go to school anyway. After the flu, they are back at school even before their stamina has fully returned. When you ask them, "What are you doing here," they say, "I don't know. I really should be home."

This is also the case when a teacher feels the next day's challenges are just too much to bear: the feeling of being so tired in one's mind that just getting out of bed seems too big a job to tackle. No student, no program, no assignment, no obligation is in actual jeopardy if a teacher needs a day of rest and recuperation.

If the first Hippocrates rule is: "First do no harm," the first rule of teaching practice must be to honor and look after oneself. No one benefits if a teacher comes to school with only two of their six cylinders charged.

To be in good health, both physically and emotionally, means a teacher is better equipped to take on the challenges of the classroom. Teachers taking care of themselves should be one of the first of the ten commandments of teaching practice.

CONCLUSION

Given the challenging nature of the tasks of teachers, the notion that one should really, truly enjoy working with students may be too idealistic to contemplate. But consider what life would be like for teachers if they had to wrestle with feelings of trepidation, a sense of foreboding, a dread that must be overcome to face the day. Consider what such feelings communicate to students, to colleagues, to parents.

The teacher who can truly, happily, genuinely enjoy being with his or her students has several plusses in his or her repertoire. Coming to school each day is a promise, and not a threat. Students perceive that pleasure and they feel pleasure in return. They know their teacher is happy to be with them and not just putting in time until the clock signals the day is done.

One doesn't have to lack good classroom control or be weak-spirited or too lax in covering the curriculum to enjoy classroom work; one doesn't have to sacrifice any element of good, successful teaching to find pleasure in the tasks. The short version is: if you are not enjoying what you are doing, perhaps teaching is not actually for you.

Chapter 5

The Teacher and the Kids

She steals into the room quietly, hoping no one will notice. Her hood covers not only her head but a part of her face. It is already fifteen past the hour; she shuffles silently to her desk, sits, and puts her head down. The teacher sees and makes note of it. This is not the first time she has been late, nor will it be the last. Reprimanding her is counterproductive; her mother insists that it is her job to get up during the night to attend to her baby sister. Consequently, Adrianna rarely gets a full night's sleep; she is tired throughout the day and can barely do her work. She is embarrassed by her lateness; she's the last person to be chosen for team or group work.

She is only one student in a class of mixed fifth and sixth graders who presents a challenging learning problem for the teacher. In that same class:

Gary is tall and limber for his age, an accomplished sports player and everyone wants him on their team. He has great difficulty with his math, so much so that he is unable to compute even the simplest addition and subtraction facts. Every strategy the teacher has tried with him has failed. It's as if he has "number blindness."

Lenny avoids doing any assigned task. Instead, he is either drawing his cartoons, "The Fabulous Four," or chipping away on a hardened piece of clay. His desk is surrounded by a sea of gray dust.

Rick hides in the reading corner, under the table. If not asked to return to his seat, he would likely be hiding away there for the entire morning. He attacks each assignment as if it were a maze through which he had to find the clue, the right pathway. School work seems a huge mystery to him.

Curtis and Mark are both engaged in "dissing" Mike, who is the only black boy in the class. They don't want him in their group. They find all sorts of reasons, nothing to do with his color, for that would surely point to their racism.

Joe is telling some of the other boys of his thefts from the local super drug store. His mother encourages him to go to the store and "cop" some nail polish for her. He brags about having done this and getting away without being caught.

Mitchell's challenge is that he is unable to read. Although he has obvious intelligence and is otherwise smart, he is unable to decipher the simplest words. He cannot remember, from one page to the next, the word he has just learned. His reading level is below Grade 1.

These are some of the boys and girls in a "normal" heterogeneous intermediate grade class in northern California. And according to the recent work of Levine (2020), the anxieties of today's parents have become a large contributor to the increase in mental health disorders of their children.

Mrs. "X" reports that she is a "Title 1" high school teacher in a school serving largely low-income, high-needs students. "By needs, I mean any and all needs you can imagine, from pregnancy to family drama. The school has only one social worker, who is stretched thin and unable to address even the most minor of the problems these students face every day of their lives. I often fall asleep at night worrying about them" (in Appiah, 2020).

The evidence of alcoholism, drug use, sexual activity, teenage pregnancy, crime, and the nefarious influences of social media that are seen in classrooms across the country are manifest in a variety of classroom behaviors and learning problems facing teachers with limited outside-of-classroom resources to deal adequately with them. What's a teacher to do?

TEACHER AS DIAGNOSTICIAN

Dealing with the presenting behaviors of students that are evidence of their academic and emotional problems is one of the most complex and demanding of the professional tasks of a teacher. Trying to figure out what a student is "telling" us with his or her behavior, interpreting it and making sense of it, and following up with the appropriate and necessary instructional strategies is sufficient to tax a veteran teacher, let alone one who has little or no classroom experience.

Standing in front of neatly aligned rows of silent students "giving a lesson" may give the illusion of "teaching." It is one way to be blinded to the individual differences, the varied learning styles, the many emotional, physical, and social learning problems that are part and parcel of the developmental levels of each of the students in a single classroom. Tackling each as an individual learner is the teacher's challenge. No one said it was easy.

Yet, if the teacher's primary job is to educate every student, there must be some strategies that can be used that are more reliable in confronting some of the impediments that lie behind students' learning difficulties. While none of what is being suggested in this chapter is a surefire guarantee of success, the teaching strategies may, at the very least, open minds to some options that might address the individual differences in learning that, in fact, exist.

What is required is not unlike a general practitioner's job in the medical clinic, who not only uses the tools of the trade (stethoscope, sphygmomanometer, thermometer) but also uses observation, touch, and listening skills to gather more data, to make some beginning determinations of what is ailing a patient. These initial examinations may lead to prescriptions for medications, for diet, for an exercise regimen, or, in more acute cases, for referral to a specialist for further treatment.

This kind of "diagnosis" is what is being suggested in dealing with individual learning difficulties. However, a word of caution: to "treat" before an informed diagnosis is made may be as futile as waiting for Godot.

As with the general practitioner, the teacher begins by observing evidence of a student's behavior in the classroom. This is followed by gathering data that supplement those observations. Then, a working hypothesis is generated that attempts to explain, to the teacher's satisfaction, what some causative factors contributing to the problem might be. Once that hypothesis is made, it should lead to a course of action, that is, teaching strategies that are based on the data gathered.

The strategies in use are also monitored to see if there is evidence that they are working; whether they are, in fact, effective; whether they need to be adjusted; or if they need to be scrapped. Keeping an ongoing record of the strategies used and the student's responses is a guide to further action.

Observing. What counterproductive behavior has been observed that gets in the way of the student's learning? How would the behavior be described, without attribution, without condemnation, without value judgments, without malice? In other words, clinically and professionally?

Gathering data. In conversations with the student, how does the student perceive what lies behind his or her difficulties? What can the student tell you about the background of his or her difficulties? In conversations with parents, what can they tell you about what they perceive to be impediments to the student's learning?

Suggesting hypotheses. Based on the data gathered from students' presenting behaviors and the information from interviews with parents and the student and perhaps with former teachers as well, what hypothesis can be suggested to explain what is going wrong? In other words, is the learning problem suggestive of unmet emotional needs? Acute anxiety? Lack of experience with thinking skills? Dyslexia? Poor coordination? Poor physical health? Sleep loss? Poor diet? Intellectual deficiencies? Auditory or visual problems? Is the student bored because the work is beneath his or her level of competence? Or any combination of factors?

Teaching strategies. Once an identification is made of the probable causative factors, appropriate teaching strategies can be identified and applied. In extreme cases, for example, where there is evidence of abuse, drugs, special needs, medical problems, a hypothesis may lead to a referral to an outside specialist. All of this is aided and abetted by the teacher's informed working hypothesis. Of course, in schools where policies of inclusion incorporate special needs students into mainstream classes, a special teacher may be provided to offer instruction and other support.

Keeping a record. With many students in a classroom, it is difficult to keep track of each individual without careful record keeping. This is especially true in cases where specific learning problems are in evidence and the teacher is engaging in an ongoing intervention plan to address those problems. Keeping brief but factual accounts of what is being done, and especially, the behaviors that are observed daily, is an important resource for the teacher, not only in terms of monitoring the success of the applications but also to point to the need for changes in strategies.

IDENTIFYING STUDENTS SHOWING EXTREME EMOTIONAL NEEDS

The work of Louis E. Raths (1998; 1978; 1986) has been helpful to many teachers seeking ways to address students' emotional needs that are impediments to learning. His groundbreaking research provided help for many teachers struggling with student behaviors that were resistant to admonition and disciplinary measures and persisted as obstacles to learning. What Raths suggested in his "theory of emotional needs" was that certain needs-related dysfunctional behaviors would be amenable to certain teaching strategies and would, eventually, diminish over time, given effective teacher interventions.

Needs Theory. Raths (1963, 1998) has written that every teacher has to deal with students who are emotionally upset and overly anxious, some more seriously so than others. While many of us, students and adults, may experience distress over a particular incident and reveal behavior related to that distress, these are not acute, nor do they persevere. On the other hand, there are students whose distress may be so intense, so acute, so extreme that their dysfunctional behaviors not only persevere but are severe impediments to learning.

Students showing such behaviors, when physical and medical problems have been ruled out, are likely indicating extreme anxieties related to feelings of insecurity.

These behaviors are seen in several forms:

Aggressiveness. These behaviors may be seen in the language of violence and/or in violence toward others or toward property. For example, name-calling, swearing, talking of what harm they are going to do to others, bragging, bullying. In their actions, aggressive students may push, wrestle, hit, slap, punch, kick, throw things at others. Sometimes they may carry weapons. They may do damage to property, like their desks or chairs, or deface bathroom walls. Sometimes they show extreme cruelty to animals.

Submissiveness. Another behavior indicative of high anxiety is the student who is very submissive, who has little sense of direction. These students seem to be unable to function independently. They seek advice and help for what to do and how to do it. Extremely submissive students are very timid and extremely hesitant about trying anything new, afraid to meet strangers, rarely able to defend themselves when picked on by others, quite easily frightened, unable to protest. It is as if all of their impulses have been dimmed by fear.

Withdrawing behavior. Very withdrawn students are not submissive; rather, they tend toward being solitary, shunning contact with others. Withdrawn students will work or play by themselves, are rarely chosen to be part of a group, are not chosen for games. They may be seen walking to school alone, rarely, if ever, in the company of their peers. These are the students who at recess will be off in a corner by themselves, never a part of the games and activities of others. They are more likely to choose a seat in the classroom that further isolates them from the rest of the group.

Psychosomatic symptoms of illness. The research on the relationship between emotional distress and psychosomatic symptoms of illness goes back at least seventy years, to the work of Flanders Dunbar (1948). As knowledge in this area has grown, it has given rise to more current work, but it has, since Dunbar's time, not been far from the thinking of the helping professions that psychosomatic illness originates from emotional distress and manifests in the body as physical pain and other symptoms.

In classrooms these behaviors may be seen in respiratory illness, asthma, other allergies; digestive problems; and gastrointestinal problems. Some students show symptoms of "accidentitis" (Dunbar, 1948), who are accident repeaters. Raths is quick to point out that students showing such symptoms should, at the very first, be seen by a medical doctor, to rule out any physical causative factor. When physical causation has been overruled, it may be possible to hypothesize the cause rooted in emotional distress.

In the classic study conducted by Fleming (1951), a group of teachers used Raths' strategies to address the incidence of psychosomatic illnesses in several of the students in their classrooms. Working along with a medical doctor who both diagnosed the students and recorded his observations of behavioral changes, Fleming revealed that "as teachers became sensitive to the nature of emotional needs, and as they attempted to meet specific needs of individual children having psychosomatic manifestations, significant improvement in the child's health occurred. This was seen in a reduction in both intensity and frequency of illness and made for improved school attendance."

Teachers considering these descriptions should be reminded that Raths is referring to behaviors seen in acute and persevering states, not as single or isolated incidents. He also reminds teachers that once observed, the first course of action is to rule out any other factors that might be contributors to the behavior—for example, any sign of illness, visual or auditory problems, malnutrition, sleeplessness, or any other medical problem. Once such determinations have been made, the teacher may then consider the classroom strategies that have, according to the research of other teachers, been effective interventions.

TEACHING STRATEGIES FOR DEALING WITH EMOTIONAL NEEDS

When students are presenting behaviors that are indicative of emotional stress, anxiety, and extreme insecurity, Raths (1998) suggests some "do's" that teachers might employ or reject that would lessen that stress and anxiety and contribute to the students' feelings of greater security. None of these is beyond the realm of expertise of any teacher, but it is important that they become an integral part of what teachers do.

While these are presented below as a "laundry list of 'do's," at best, they should be natural expressions of a teacher's intention to show care, respect, and consideration for the student and what the student is experiencing. These are not necessarily "instructional strategies" but rather a teacher's way of "being" with the students, of finding opportunities to ensure that they feel safe and more secure and relating to them as caring adults.

Providing them with a chance to disclose some of their anxieties and responding with empathy, warmth, and genuineness would be high on the list of "to do's."

What is also important is for the teacher to remember that these are not quick fixes; in other words, they are not miracle cures. Some of the counterproductive behaviors that students have formed in response to distress have become deeply embedded in their personae, so it is likely that it will require a good deal of time for teachers using these strategies to see positive change. In other words, don't give up; don't despair; don't lose hope.

- When a student has been absent from school, make sure to make him or her feel welcome on his or her return.

- Maintain a warm, respectful, and genuine relationship with all students.
- Show appreciation for their efforts.
- Appreciate their individuality, their differences.
- Make it safe for them to make mistakes without suggesting they are failures.
- Ensure that no child is excluded from any activity.
- Avoid punishing students that embarrass or humiliate them.
- Prize their achievements. But be honest about offering positive feedback.
- Beware of stressing rewards; they often create a hostile sense of competition.
- Avoid insisting that all students conform to one standard of time, with respect to finishing their work.
- Ensure that the tasks and activities are easily understood and within the realm of students' competence.
- Avoid making too many judgments about a student's progress. Ensure that judgments are honest and respectful.
- When students are required to pay for certain activities (like a field trip, or extra curriculum activities), be careful not to embarrass students who lack the funds.
- Allow students to approach you with their concerns. Give them opportunities to come to you to speak openly about their feelings. Reassure them when they need encouragement.
- Respect their choices, insofar as possible.
- Be respectful of students' concerns no matter how odd they may sound.
- When deep psychological problems emerge, make sure to call on a professional who is equipped to deal with them.
- When a student is "acting out," be sure to differentiate that your response is to the behavior and not to the student.
- Rejecting any student because of his or her behavior should be avoided at all costs.
- Be a human person to your students. Leave your "professional falsetto" at the classroom door.
- Try not to be overwhelmed by negative behavior. Try to be sympathetic to their causes.
- Even when you are stretched to the limits of your endurance, try to avoid shaming, humiliating, and debasing students for what they have done.
- Try to be accepting when students want to take issue with something you have said or done. Allow them to voice their opinions in the absence of your criticisms.
- If you feel the extreme need to mete out a punishment, make sure that what you do is fair, honest, and consonant with the offending behavior.

And to sum: never, ever, ever make a student feel less able, less happy, less secure at the end of a school day than at the beginning. If a student feels diminished, then you have harmed him or her, rather than taught.

IDENTIFYING BEHAVIOR THAT RELATES TO LACK OF EXPERIENCE WITH THINKING

One of the persistent and nagging counterproductive behaviors of students is seen in behaviors that reveal their lack of experience with the higher-order mental processes. It is often assumed that developing thinking skills is by-product of subject matter learning. Alas, the data reveal that that is far from the case. As with other skills that need focused instruction so do higher-order thinking skills.

Louis E. Raths (1966) spent more than 1,000 hours working with classroom teachers observing students' behavior. His field research enabled him to generate a theory of thinking that has permitted teachers to understand the link between inadequate development of cognitive skills and student behavior.

The theory suggests that certain behaviors, seen persistently and in the extreme, may be a sign that students have had insufficient opportunities to develop their higher-order mental skills. The theory also suggests that if teachers were to provide these students with focused instruction on higher-order mental tasks, these maladaptive behaviors would diminish over time and be replaced by more thoughtful ways of behaving (Raths, Wassermann, Jonas, & Rothstein, 1986; Wassermann, 2009).

Embedded in the descriptions of these behaviors is the nature of what is "wanting" as students struggle to master the higher-order tasks that are part and parcel of a developing acquaintance with thought.

- Extreme impulsiveness: jumps to conclusions or resolutions before the data are clear
- Overdependence on others, for example, the teacher, another adult, a more skilled student
- Inability to concentrate on more demanding tasks: attention easily diverted from what needs to be done
- Missing the meaning: unable to find the nuggets of what's important in a story, an essay, a lecture, a book
- Extreme dogmatism: the belief that one's own view is right and good while all others are faulty or not worth consideration
- Inflexibility: rigidity about one's position, unable to see nuances or alternate points of view

- Lack of confidence in one's own thinking: unable to come to grips with higher-order cognitive demands
- Unwillingness to think: puts a value judgment on "thinking" as a nonessential skill

Once again, a diagnosis is made on the basis of observations of such behaviors seen in acute and persevering patterns, not as infrequent episodes of frustration or lack of interest in a task. And once again, a hypothesis can be formed when other factors, such as physical problems, have been ruled out.

TEACHING STRATEGIES FOR DEALING WITH LACK OF EXPERIENCE WITH THINKING

In the past two dozen years, several professionals have offered counsel about how teachers may go about "teaching for thinking" in their elementary and secondary classrooms, some of whom suggest "thinking" as a separate area of study to be included as part of the curriculum (Costa, 1985; Paul & Elder, 2002; Pogrow, 2005; Segal, Chipman & Glasser, 1985; Sternberg, 1987). Where Raths differs from them is in his advocacy that curriculum tasks be developed with an eye and ear to how they, themselves, can promote intelligent thinking.

Thinking, then, is not a separate field of study but rather integral to how a curriculum task is shaped. Raths offers specific strategies for how this is done—that is, by incorporating higher-order mental operations into the curriculum task. These "operations" serve as a basis for developing curriculum tasks (Raths et al, 1986). The operations include:

- Comparing
- Interpreting data
- Observing
- Summarizing
- Classifying
- Making decisions
- Suggesting hypotheses
- Imagining and creating
- Criticizing and evaluating
- Designing projects and investigations
- Applying principles in new situations
- Gathering and organizing data
- Coding to become aware of certain patterns of thinking

A cursory examination of these mental operations reveals that each requires a student to do "something more" with information, something more than merely absorbing it from a page and recalling facts. This "more" involves more sophisticated and intelligent examination of that information, leading to increased understanding of the important ideas (Wassermann, 2009).

An example of how this is done:

The teacher has planned a science investigation in which the students (Grade 4) will be studying skins in order to observe their properties and functions.

The big idea underlying this investigation is:

Animal skins function primarily for protection. Skin is a growing organ. It has color (pigmentation) and comes in layers. It may have hair, feathers, or scales.

The thinking operations included in the students' investigations are:

Observing, comparing, classifying and interpreting data, examining assumptions, suggesting hypotheses, designing investigations, making decisions, evaluating.

The curriculum task involves several stages:

1. **Investigative Play**—in which students, working in small groups, conduct scientific inquiries with a prepared group of materials.
2. **Debriefing**—follows the investigative play, in which the teacher, working with the full group, raises higher-order questions to further students' thinking about their observations and investigations.
3. **Extending**—follows the debriefing, in which the students return to their investigations and pursue additional inquiries spurred on by the teacher's questions.

Investigative Play:

The teacher has provided each investigative play group with the following materials:

> A variety of skins including fruit skins (apple, banana, orange, grape, mango, coconut, pear, melon), vegetable skins (potato, onion, carrot, squash, tomato), nut skins (peanut, almond, sunflower seeds, filberts), and animal skins (pieces of leather, molted reptile skins, pieces of fur); small knives, magnifying lenses, microscope.

Each investigative play group is supplied with an Activity Card:

- Use the materials in this center to conduct some investigations about skin.
- In what ways are the skins alike? How are they different?

- Make some observations about strength, texture, hardness or softness, edibility, color, shape, smell, and function.
- Talk with each other about your observations.
- Then, make some notes about what you have discovered.

Debriefing:
The teacher has prepared the following questions to be used in the follow-up activity to the investigative play:

- What observations have you made about skin in general?
- What observations have you made about the strength of skin? The texture? Its hardness or softness? Its color? Its edibility? Its shape? Its smell?
- What kinds of living things have skin? Can you give some examples?
- In what ways might these skins be grouped?
- What do you suppose skin is good for? What hypotheses can you suggest?
- What are some differences between animal skins and plant skins?
- Why do you suppose some animals shed their skins? How is this done? What are your ideas about it?
- Which skins are more attractive? What is there about them that makes them attractive? What are your ideas about this?

Extending:
The teacher plans to extend the students' investigations after the debriefing with the following kinds of activities:

- By adding new materials to the investigations, for example, feathers, hair, fish skins, chicken skin, chicken feet, crab, shrimp, oyster, or mussel shells.
- By introducing new activity cards, for example: compare feathers and leathers. How are they alike? How are they different?
- By asking students to conduct new investigations to see the relationship between skin and hair.
- By asking students to conduct new investigations to compare human skin and chicken skin, banana skin, onion skin. (Reprinted by permission of the Publisher. From Selma Wassermann and J. W. George Ivany, *The New Teaching Elementary Science Who's Afraid of Spiders*, 2nd Edition. New York: Teachers College Press. Copyright © 1996. By Teachers College, Columbia University. All rights reserved.)

Much more about developing curriculum activities will be found in chapter 9.

OTHER BEHAVIOR IMPEDIMENTS TO LEARNING

Not all students' dysfunctional behaviors are covered by the Raths's Needs and Thinking theories. There are those that lie outside the realm of thinking and needs-related behaviors that are troublesome for the teacher, for the other students, and for the student himself or herself. These may require interventions and teaching strategies that are idiosyncratic to each special situation. Obviously not all of them can be addressed in this chapter, but some suggestions are made that may be helpful to teachers who are searching for ways to inform their actions.

Students who have the intelligence but fail to achieve in subject areas, specifically reading and math, may require individual teaching programs to enable them to make some progress in these realms. One of the mitigating factors in such disabilities is that students who struggle with these academics may have already built up a "failure syndrome" in which they have convinced themselves that they are stupid and unable to learn. This must be overcome in teaching them, alongside with tangible evidence of their success. It is by showing them that they "can do" that they are able to overcome their sense of failure and make progress.

One of the more helpful texts in the area of reading disability is Albert Harris's *How to Increase Reading Ability*. Originally written in 1945, it was followed by nine new editions and is valuable for its practical and specific suggestions for both diagnosing and providing help for students who struggle with reading problems.

Constance Kamill's (1994; 1980) work in math education offers ideas and teaching strategies that enable mathematical understanding and skill development. She recommends math games and, of course, hands-on manipulatives to aid and abet mathematical understanding.

CONCLUSION

It takes a lot of grit, know how, perseverance, and willingness to tackle the mega challenges of dealing with the counterproductive behaviors of students. Of course, not all students in a given class would need that kind of specialized treatment. But for those that do, it is folly to abandon them to methods that are beyond their abilities, their emotional stability, their particular dysfunctionalities. For such neglect leads only to more and persistent failure, a legacy of indifference to the troubles that these students face now and in their future.

So why should a teacher take on this kind of challenge, given all else that is demanded of him or her in a teaching day? Not only for the satisfaction of helping students in dire need but also for the pleasure, the absolute and delightful joy, that primal sense of satisfaction that comes from seeing a student who is working to overcome his or her difficulties, making unambiguous and remarkable progress. When a teacher can observe that she or he has helped a student to reach goals that student thought never able to obtain, the pleasure of witnessing our own achievements cannot be overestimated.

And that is why we do it.

Chapter 6

Teacher-Student Interactions

"You can hear a lot by just listening."

—*Yogi Berra*

He stands with his nose pressed against the glass of the fish tank. The lion fish, with their porcupine-like dorsal fins and warrior faces, swim indifferently past him, ignoring the small cloud of his breath on the window. He is so fascinated by these sea creatures and their spectacular colors that he has forgotten his classmates and his teacher, who are taking off for another part of the aquarium. His teacher looks back, sees him there, and calls, "Hey, William. We're ready to move on now." Reluctantly he separates himself from the glass and moves slowly over to where the rest of his sixth-grade class is waiting.

"I wuz watchin' the lion fish, Miz Camrose. They got those spikes on their backs."

Which one of at least a hundred different ways of responding will the teacher choose in replying to William? How will that response affect William's sense of personal power? His appreciation for lion fish? His emotional health? His attitude toward school and his teacher? How will the teacher's response encourage William's interest in the life of the sea? In the miracles of marine biology?

These questions lie at the heart of teacher-student interactions, for different ways of responding to students have different effects upon their thinking, their sense of personal power, their attitudes about school and teachers, their emotional health, and, of course, their interest in a particular subject area. And a teacher's response can be for better or for worse, helpful or hurtful, additive or subtractive. Using responses that enable and empower students, that build students' self-esteem and their healthy attitudes about school and learning, is one more sophisticated and challenging function of teachers. If designing relevant and developmentally sound curriculum experiences is the top side of a teacher's job, the use of appropriate interactive skills is the underbelly. It takes two to tango.

Classroom teachers interact with their students hundreds of times each day, and each day they choose from an extensive repertoire of possibilities: responses that attend to students' learning needs, to behavior, to organizational and management matters, to students' ideas. These responses are formulated quickly and often in rapid succession within the give and take of dozens of verbal interchanges.

This interactive process, intense and demanding, asks a lot of the teacher: to respond thoughtfully, appropriately, and sensitively in ways that are helpful and not hurtful, when the environment is charged with activity and other institutional demands. It is no wonder that teachers feel exhausted at the end of each teaching day. The interactive process of teaching alone demands great energy, considered thought, and the highest level of professional functioning.

In whatever ways teachers respond to students, those responses impart explicit and implicit messages. A response has power to hurt or to help. It has power to be psychologically additive or subtractive: to empower or disempower, to enhance or diminish thinking, to open minds to new understanding or not. Teachers' responses can be inviting, appreciative, respectful. They can be rejecting, cruel, punishing. They can foster autonomy, or they can cultivate dependency. They can build more excitement about learning or they can demolish students' interest in the subject.

Perhaps this seems like overegging the pudding, assigning too much weight to statements people make to each other. But it is impossible to sell short the potential effects of the ways in which people respond to each other, the ways in which teachers respond to students.

Given that teachers have hundreds of options tucked away in their "response repertoires," which one of the many may be chosen to respond to William, the eleven-year-old who tarried with the lion fish while the rest of his class went on to another part of the aquarium? As in most other decisions teachers make, it depends. It depends on whether the teacher wants to address William's behavior or his thinking. In either case, certain guidelines apply.

At the very first, a response should be respectful of a student's feelings about self. It should never demean or diminish. At best, it should empower, promote a student's autonomy, rather than foster dependence. The response should also attend to what the student has said. The student must know that the teacher has heard him or her. When at least these conditions can be met, almost any response, whether it addresses behavior or learning, will be helpful, both psychologically and academically additive.

If Miss Camrose, William's teacher, chooses to address William's behavior, she has several options that incorporate the guidelines of respecting, empowering, and attending to William's situation. For example:

"I know you were very interested in those lion fish, William. But I was worried that you might get separated from the class and we would lose you."

Or: "Those lion fish were fascinating. I can understand that you wanted to watch them for a long time. I know it's hard for you to come away when you would prefer to stay here."

Both responses are respectful of William's self and his interests. They both attend to what he has said. Both tell him that his option to remain with the fish has been foreclosed. Yet, they do so with consideration. In that way, they are both additive and empowering. Examples of alternatives that are disrespectful, and therefore diminishing, include the following:

"We don't have time for that now, William."
"They have, William. Not got. Have. Can you say, 'They have?'"
"We've all been waiting for you, William. It wasn't nice of you to keep us waiting."

If Miss Camrose wants to take the time to engage William's thinking about the lion fish, she also has options available in which the criteria of respect, attending, and empowering are evident. For example:

"Those spikes stick right up on the top of the fish. They make the fish look very menacing."

"Those spikes seem to be very sharp. I wonder if a person could get hurt by touching them."

"You were very interested in those lion fish. I can understand it. They are beautiful and ugly at the same time."

All three of the above engage William's thinking. They ask him to reflect on what he has seen, to think a little more about what he has observed. Each attends to his statement and each respects his idea, as well as attends to the student as an observer.

Or, conversely, the teacher's responses might include nonrespectful, nonattending, disempowering statements as well. For example:

"What's the correct name for those spikes, William?" In this question the "label" or correct answer is more important than asking William to think more about his observation or about the function of the dorsal fins. William's observation is disregarded. If he should know the name, he will have only the momentary satisfaction of "getting it right" and pleasing the teacher.

Or: "Yes, that's the spinous dorsal fin. Lion fish are bony fish and they have two dorsal fins, one of them spinous, like spikes, you see. They flutter and in that way help the fish move through the water, which is the function of that dorsal fin. They are very sharp to the touch and that gives the fish protection from its enemies, like porcupine quills. The lion fish also carry venom in their spinous dorsal fins, like a poisonous snake. So if you were to touch one of those spikes, or step on one, the poison is apt to hurt you badly."

In this response, the teacher talks too much and gives William more data than he is likely to be able to absorb in that moment. The teacher disempowers William by taking control of the action and reducing William from active participant observer to passive listener.

Or, "What are they for, William? You remember. We learned that yesterday in class."

In this statement the teacher ignores William's observation and instead focuses on the function of the dorsal fin as well as asking him to give her the right answer. If William can remember, he will be rewarded and have some satisfaction in knowing that he has pleased the teacher. If he does not remember, he will feel diminished.

How teachers interact with students not only has profound effects on student learning. It also contributes to the quality of life in classrooms.

And that's only the beginning.

IT STARTS WITH LISTENING, ATTENDING, AND APPREHENDING

"When was the last time you really listened to someone? Really listened without thinking about what you wanted to say next, glancing down at your phone or jumping in to offer your opinion?" writes Kate Murphy (2020) in a recent edition of the *New York Times*. "Bad listeners interrupt, stare at their cellphones, divert their eyes to someone or something else; the sad truth is that people have more experience being cut off, ignored and misunderstood than heard. If people are listening to anything, it's likely through headphones or earbuds. This is fueling what public health officials describe as an epidemic of loneliness" (Murphy, 2020).

Where and how do people learn good listening skills? And why is that important? To the latter question, the answer is obvious and that is especially true in the classroom. Students who are listened to respectfully, thoughtfully, and sympathetically know from these interactions that they are cared about and that what they say has value. Students who are ignored, whose responses are dismissed, learn that who they are and what they say have no value. This is a poor lesson to take away from one's in-school experience.

But there is more: a teacher who is able to listen, to attend, to apprehend what a student is saying is being offered the "working material" that can enable that student's learning and growth. There is a huge payoff for good listening skills.

However, it's not enough to listen. Listening for meaning, both to the surface of the statement and to what lies behind it, requires "attending," being fully focused on what is being said. When listening and attending are both present, the teacher is then able to apprehend—making meaning of the totality of what the student is saying. This "meaning making" allows for greater understanding and provides the teacher with the data from which an appropriate response can be constructed.

The skills of listening, attending, and apprehending begin with the teacher turning his and her full attention to the student. Body language, facial expression, and eyes all give the message: "I am listening to what you have to say. What you have to say is important to me."

Attending means shutting out all other sounds and concentrating fully on what the student is saying. It is more than just hearing the words. It involves observing the behavioral cues as the words are being spoken, the nuances, the voice inflection, the words chosen to express certain ideas, noticing where a statement or word is given emphasis. When all of that occurs in listening and attending, the teacher is doing what Freire (1983) calls "apprehending." This understanding provides the working material for the teacher's response.

How do teachers new to this kind of work begin to listen, attend, and apprehend? It starts with a conscious effort to tune into the what and the how of a student's statements. It requires that the teacher free his or her mind, so that it is open to hear and observe, for one cannot listen and attend if one is, at the same moment, thinking of something else. Nothing may get in the way of full concentration on the student and what the student is saying.

Texts offering advice on the development of such interpersonal skills (Brammer, 1979; Carkhuff & Berenson, 1983) suggest that the ability to attend thoughtfully and intelligently increases as the following conditions are met:

- Making and holding eye contact with the student
- Listening to and communicating respect for the student's idea
- Being free from the need to evaluate the student's idea, in either word or tone
- Avoiding reactive comment on the student's idea
- Avoiding offering one's own ideas
- Being aware of affect (verbal or nonverbal) being communicated
- Being especially aware of indicators of stress
- Being able to make the student feel safe, nondefensive, and nonthreatened throughout the dialogue[1]

The teacher's ability to listen, attend, and apprehend provides him or her with the information needed to formulate appropriate responses. It also creates the climate in which respect for students and for their ideas is palpable and makes it safe for them to offer them. Even more, it contributes to the essential conditions of the interactive dialogue—that is, the teacher and the students engaging in a discussion in which all parties together are attempting to understand.

The teacher's skill in listening, attending, and apprehending is basic to masterful teaching, to the interconnectivity of humanness and teaching. It is on this foundation that all other interactive skills rest.

CHOOSING THE RIGHT RESPONSE

As mentioned above in the mini-scenario played out with William and Ms. Camrose, there are many ways in which teachers respond to students, depending on several factors. Should the response be about behavior? Or should it be about asking the student to think more deeply about the issues? Or should it give information? Or should it make a judgment? Or?

Choosing the "right" response is a reflection of the teacher's purpose. What's important is that the purpose is clear, and the response works to further that purpose.

The bottom line is that there is no "right" answer, no response that "correctly" fits all situations. No response is "wrong" if it meets the criteria of being respectful of the student's sense of self and of the student's idea. How the teacher responds is a reflection of where the teacher wants to go with the issues being raised by the student.

Not all students' statements are about curriculum or issues related to curriculum. Some give voice to feelings and personal concerns, and these ask for more empathic responses that address those feelings. Once again, no response is "wrong" if it is respectful of the student: that is, if the student is heard, attended to, the meaning is apprehended, and the response addresses all of that in reply.

Basic Reflective Responses

The safest and perhaps most basic of all interactive responses is the reflective response. These are "basic" because they are fundamental to the interactive process. They communicate to a student that the teacher has "heard" their statement; they hold a verbal mirror to what the student has said so that he or she has an opportunity to reexamine it from a new perspective.

These responses are inviting in their own way; students know they are being listened to and thus feel safe about offering further ideas. They have the power to build trust in the teacher-student relationship, thus opening an opportunity for further reflection.

Some basic responses:

- Saying the idea back in some new way
- Paraphrasing the idea
- Interpreting the idea

Example from Grade 4

Ivy: I don't see why we can't use our tablets in class to help us figure out things. Mr. Slattery's class is allowed to use them.

Teacher: You think that you should be able to bring your tablets to school and use them to help you with your work. (*Paraphrases*)

Ivy: Yeah. It's not fair if one class can use them and we can't.

Teacher: You'd like all fourth graders to use the same materials. That is, if Mr. Slattery's class can use tablets, then you should be able to use them too. (*Interprets*)

Ivy: Yeah. Why should we have to suffer? Tablets could help us.

Teacher: You think it's a matter of suffering. It's harder to do work without the help of tablets. (*Paraphrases*)

Ivy: Tablets could help us. You should change that rule.

Teacher: You'd like me to change the rule so that everyone who has a tablet can bring it to school and use it to help with their work. (*Paraphrase*)

Teacher: I'd like to hear what some of the other students have to say about it. Thanks, Ivy, for giving us your thoughts on it.

Example from Grade 10

Milton: Global warming is an important issue. I think that those government leaders who ignore it are reckless and irresponsible.

Teacher: You've raised the issue of global warming as one that should be first on our list of what needs to be done. Our government leaders need to play a role in addressing this issue. (*Paraphrase*)

Milton: Yeah. We could all do something about it. We could each play a role.

Teacher: All of us, even our Grade 10 social studies class, could take some responsibility for helping to move this issue forward. (*Interprets*)

Milton: More than that. We could do more than that. We could be proactive ourselves.

Teacher: You'd like to see all of us, students included, take an active role by doing something more to deal with climate change. (*Paraphrases*)

Milton: Yeah. And I have some ideas about that.

Teacher: I'd like to hear about them, Milton.

While on the surface it may seem that these "basic" responses that paraphrase or interpret students' statements may not be adequate to move the discussion forward in a productive examination of issues. However, experience has shown that this is far from the case. They should not be underestimated in their ability to generate productive examination of issues.

Moreover, they explicitly and implicitly communicate not only respect for students' ideas but also demonstrate that the teacher is "tuned in" and cares about what students are saying. Nor to be underestimated is their capacity to contribute to a safe classroom discussion; no student needs to feel threatened, harshly judged, or challenged confrontationally in the presence of these basic responses.

Responses that Call for Analysis of Ideas

At a more challenging level are responses that call for students to analyze the ideas they are expressing. Such responses ask for deeper examination and go beyond surface observations. These include:

- Asking for examples
- Asking if assumptions are being made
- Asking if alternatives have been considered
- Asking for supporting data
- Asking how the student arrived that idea

This is not an exhaustive list of what may be asked, but it offers some suggestions about the kinds of questions that can be used in asking students to dig more deeply into the statements they are making. Unlike "basic" responses, these are often framed as questions; basic responses are more often framed as statements. That is one reason that they are more cognitively challenging. Each requires the student to take his or her idea further, to examine what has been said from some new perspective.

Once again, as is the case in using reflective responses, each question calling for analysis is put respectfully, in words used and in tone of voice, so that a student does not feel under attack. The *sine qua* non is that the student is being invited to participate in a thoughtful examination of his or her ideas.

It is also important to note that when responses calling for analyses are used, they are used in combination with basic responses.

Example from a Grade 2 Class

Gwen: I know that you can get a cold from catching someone's germs.

Teacher: You have some ideas about how people can catch a cold. (*Paraphrases*) Germs are passed from person to person and you can catch a cold that way. (*Interprets*)

Gwen: That's how I got a cold. I caught it from my brother.

Teacher: You think you got some germs from your brother and you caught his cold. (*Paraphrases*) I wonder how you figured that out? (Asks how the student arrived at that idea)

Gwen: I just figured it out myself. It's my idea.

Teacher: Your brain told you. That's the way you figure things out. (*Interprets*)

Gwen: But sometimes I learned it from TV. They tell you not to cough or sneeze without a tissue because that way the germs fly all over the place and someone else can catch it.

Teacher: Sometimes you learn something from watching TV. I wonder if you can trust the announcers on TV to tell you the truth? What do you think about that? (*Paraphrases; asks if assumptions are being made*)

Example from Grade 8

Ilya: I think we need to be careful about what we are posting on Facebook and Instagram. People can follow you and sometimes that's fun, but it can be dangerous.

Teacher: You see some advantages to posting material on Facebook and Instagram, but you also see some dangers. (*Interpreting*) Can you give me some examples, Ilya, of what you see as some dangers? (*Asks for examples*)

Ilya: Well, some kids post secrets and pretty soon everyone knows their secrets.

Teacher: What you post on Facebook or Instagram gets read by thousands. Can you give us an idea of how this is dangerous? (*Paraphrases; asks for examples*)

Ilya: I guess it's OK if you want the world to know all about you. But suppose you did something bad and you posted it on Facebook, then everyone in the world would know you were bad.

Teacher: You wonder if it's a good idea to expose yourself, to allow the world to know your secrets. (*Interprets*) Thanks so much, Ilya. I wonder if anyone else has an idea to share on this issue?

As can be seen in the above examples, the teacher uses the reflective response in combination with responses that call for analysis. This has the function of letting the student know they are being heard; the teacher is listening. It is then followed up by a question that asks the student to dig a bit deeper in analyzing his or her statements.

Responses that Challenge

At the most demanding level of student-teacher interactions are those that call for the students' generation of new ideas. These more challenging questions and responses require the student to extend his or her thinking into new, uncharted territory; to come up with ideas that go beyond what has already been said; and to take data and manipulate them into new configurations, so that something new and bold is revealed.

These responses are risky, because they put the student on the spot. They are used sparingly because more frequent use is more than likely to raise anxiety levels. As well, overuse has the tendency to torque the discussion into unrelated pathways, thereby losing focus of the main ideas. It is helpful to remember that it is the basic, reflective responses that ground the discussion; they enable a more careful, more studied examination of the issues.

Challenging responses are most often framed as questions:

- What hypotheses can you suggest that would explain it?
- How would you interpret that data?
- What principles can be applied from that into new situations?
- Based on what you have said, what predictions can you make about what is theoretically possible?
- How would you go about testing that theory?
- How do you see a plan of action arising from those issues?
- What decisions have you come to? And what might be some consequences of those decisions?

Example from a Grade 12 Class

Adam: The separation of the UK from the European Union I think was done as a backlash to people's fears about immigration. Britain has had open borders since they entered into the Union and it has made people a little crazy.

Teacher: You see Brexit as a response to more populist fears about immigration. (*Paraphrase*). What's more, you see the response as irrational—tell me if I have gone too far in interpreting what you have said. (*Interpreting*)

Adam: No, I think that's what I mean. It's not a thought-about action. It's more like a reaction.

Teacher: You see some potential negative consequences of it. (*Interprets*) I wonder if you could identify some of those? (*Asks for predictions*)

Adam: Well, I haven't thought that through, so perhaps I'm going off the deep end here.

Teacher: You may need some more time to think about the implications, as you see them. (*Interprets*)

Adam: Yeah. I want to give it some more thought.

Teacher: I'm going to ask others to wade in here and give their views. Yes, Debbie?

Debbie: I think those who voted in favor of Brexit haven't appreciated what it will mean to the economy if they divorce themselves from the Union.

Teacher: The British economy is likely to suffer? (*Paraphrases*). Can you give some examples of how this could happen? (*Asks for examples*)

Debbie: Well, according to what I've read, there is a good chance that trade will suffer.

Teacher: Can you suggest some hypotheses that would account for the loss in trade? (*Asks for hypotheses to be generated*)

Debbie: Well, with open borders, goods can travel freely across national borders. With Brexit, there is likely to be import taxes, export taxes, who knows what all else. All of those Brits who go through the Chunnel to buy wine more cheaply in France will have to pay higher prices to buy their wine locally.

Teacher: It will mean increases in prices for some goods that come from Europe and that might be a hardship for some people who depend on those goods. (*Paraphrases*) Thanks, Debbie. Does anyone else want to add their ideas?

Example from a Grade 3 Class

Teacher: We were talking yesterday about how the ads on TV try to persuade you to buy things that perhaps you don't even need. But the ads make you want those things badly. Does anyone want to comment about that?

Malcolm: It's not only the ads on TV. You get ads on the computer, too. Like when you are trying to look something up, an ad pops up and tells you to buy something.

Teacher: There are ads on TV but there are also ads on your computer and perhaps your tablets. (*Paraphrases and interprets*)

Malcolm: Yeah. They tell you about new apps that you just have to have for your tablet. And then you think I've got to have that app!

Teacher: The ads persuade you that you need something that you didn't even know about before. (*Interprets*)

Malcolm: Yeah and then I have to beg my mother or my father to buy it for me.

Teacher: That puts you in a hard position. You have to beg your parents to buy the app for you. (*Paraphrases*) So tell me this, Malcolm, what would happen if you didn't get the app? (*Asks for potential consequences*)

Malcolm: I'd be disappointed and I'd get into a big argument with my parents.

Teacher: And that would be one downside of the ads that try to persuade you to buy. I see. Thanks Malcolm for giving us your ideas. (*Interprets and acknowledges the student's contribution*). I'd like to hear some other ideas. Anyone else want to tell us what they think?

Before concluding this section on challenging questions, one more issue needs to be raised, and that is the use of "why?" questions, which crop up into teachers' discussions as facilely as demolishing an éclair. These "why" questions are most frequently heard as "Why do you think so?" or "Why, or why not?" The question is intended as a challenge, and its purpose is to have the student defend an idea with data.

The recommendation for a more productive interactive exchange is to use "why" questions sparingly, if at all. They are, first, highly challenging and frequently off-putting. Second, they seem to be a fallback when teachers can't think of a more appropriate question or response. So instead of "why do you think so?" perhaps:

What reasons do you have to explain it?
What data support your ideas?
What examples can you give?
"What" questions tend to give sharper focus to the inquiry and keep the discourse more on track of the big ideas. They are also less confrontational.

Responses that Address Students' Expression of Feelings

There will be occasions when a teacher's response falls outside the bailiwick of curriculum and nudges into the realm of students' feelings. Classrooms are not vacuums where only academic activities occur; they are human societies where students' feelings and needs more than often come to the surface and need a teacher's attention. It is no secret that there are students who come to school in conflict with themselves or with others, to the extent that they are unable to mobilize enough of their resources to become productive learners.

While they may not be so emotionally challenged as to be considered "severely disturbed," these students need careful consideration and skillful attention to prevent them from becoming personal and academic failures. While in most cases these students would benefit from professional psychological help, this help is not always available. Whether or not such help is offered, the classroom teacher is still left with the responsibility that comes with the student's day-to-day presence in his or her classroom.

Appropriate teacher-student interactions may go far to address them, providing emotional and nurturing support to students in need. Should teachers be called upon to respond in such ways? The answer is: how can it be avoided if a classroom is to become a place where students know they are cared for and cared about—above and beyond their school lessons?

Showing a bit of empathy for students' needs goes a long way to nurture and nourish students who come to school with a lot of "baggage" brought from home experiences that are less than satisfying, less than happy, less than emotionally sound. And if such life experiences get in the way of student learning, a teacher does have some resources that may not solve the problem but may go a long way to help a student feel that at least, in school, he or she is safe, cared about, understood. The power of empathic interactions to do good cannot be overestimated.

Once again, such interactions begin with listening, attending, and apprehending—taking in the whole of what a student is presenting as he or she opens his or her heart, unleashing a flood of emotion. Responding begins with acknowledgment that such an expression is OK; in other words, even in classrooms, strong feelings emerge. They don't go away on demand. The notion that "boys don't cry" is not only unacceptable but unsound.

- Begin, at first, by showing that you are listening, that you have tuned in to what the student is saying. Wait until the student has finished his or her statements. Don't interrupt. Use the cues suggested earlier in this chapter to show you are fully present with your attention.
- Use a response to show that you have heard, both in content and in feeling, what the student has been expressing. This is similar to the "saying back" but also includes a reflection of the student's feelings.
- Wait to hear how the student replies.
- Use another reflective response to feedback, again, the meaning of the student's statement and the feelings being expressed.
- Continue with these responses until you and the student have come to some resolution of the situation.
- Use the phrase "tell me more" when you need more information or want the student to continue explaining the problem.
- Never judge; never offer advice; never say, "You shouldn't feel that way." These are less than useless. They are counterproductive.
- Among all other things, be genuine in what you are communicating to the student; avoid "packaged" responses, like "I hear you."

These "facilitative" responses are a teacher's important tools in dealing with students in crisis or under stress. They go a long way in making a student feel more secure, less afraid, less alone. They communicate to the student that you are listening to him or her, that you have respect for the student and what the student is feeling.

It is important to recognize that these responses do not "solve" the problems a student is carrying. That is not their intent. But what they do provide is the emotional support of telling the student that you care, that he or she is not alone, that you understand.

Example from a Grade 7 Class

Craig: I'm working very hard, Ms. Day. I'm really trying. But I can't seem to get it right.

Teacher: You are having a lot of trouble with your homework assignments, Craig. (*Paraphrases*) Tell me more.

Craig: It's just that I don't have a good place at home to work. My brother is always picking on me. My mother keeps asking me to help her. Every time I sit down to work, I get interrupted.

Teacher: You can't seem to find a good place to do your work at home. Lots of interruptions from your brother. Your mother also needs your help. (*Paraphrases*)

Craig: You see, that's the trouble. How can I concentrate on my work? They are driving me crazy.

Teacher: I can see that it's making you very angry. You can't finish your work under those conditions. (*Interprets; reflects student's feelings*)

Craig: I don't know what to do. I want to do good in school. (*Begins to cry*)

Teacher: I can see how upset you are, Craig. (*Reflects feelings*) Sit down for a little while and think about how you'd like me to help. (*Gives the student some time to collect himself, and asks him to take ownership of how he'd like to have help*)

Example from a Grade 2 Class

Abbey: My mom can't come to the conference. I wanted to show her my stuff.

Teacher: You're disappointed. You wanted your mom to come to the classroom. (*Reflects feelings. Paraphrases the statement*)

Abbey: She never comes. She has to work.

Teacher: You wish she would be able to come, but her work gets in the way. (*Reflects feelings and interprets statement*)

Abbey: I wish she didn't have to work. She's always tired. She never comes to my class.

Teacher: You are so sad. You don't like it when your mom has to work so hard. (*Reflects feelings; interprets statement*)

Abbey: All the other kids' moms come. (*Begins to cry*)

Teacher: It's so hard when you want your mom to come to class and she can't make it. Sometimes it feels as if you are the only one in the class whose mom isn't coming. (*Reflects feelings; interprets statement*)

Abbey: (*Cries more*) Teacher puts arm around her to comfort her.

N.B. The problem is not resolved, but Abbey, at the least, knows her teacher understands and offers her comfort.

MASTERING THE ART OF TEACHER-STUDENT INTERACTIONS

There is no magic wand that enables a teacher to shift gears to become a master in the art of facilitative teacher-student interactions, especially when that teacher has had long and enduring experiences with telling, advising, judging, and informing as his or her modus operandi in the classroom. But it would not be facile to say that the key lies in the teacher's ability to listen to self in the act of speaking to students. Learning to tune in to what is coming out of one's mouth is the first step taken in becoming more skillful.

There are ways to do this, and teachers who wish to pursue these essential teaching strategies will surely find their own resources. It is not unlike learning to listen to oneself practicing a Chopin Etude, for example, listening for the wrong notes, the phrasing, the nuances of expression, the overall arch of the music, so that one begins to master not only the skills but the art of it. What is also essential is the teacher's ability to be nondefensive about his and her errors; defensiveness is probably the toughest stumbling block to overcome in the process of learning.

For teachers who wish to develop their facilitative skills, the bottom line is that it does involve a lifetime of learning: learning to become more adept, more sensitively tuned in, more skilled at picking out the "right" response. It is much like the concert violinist Nadja Salerno-Sonnenberg, who, after playing the Mendelssohn Violin Concerto a hundred or so times in concert, continues to practice it for hours before every subsequent performance. One never stops learning performance skills; one never stops learning teacher-student interaction skills.

It should also be noted that, despite a teacher's wish to become more facilitative in his or her teacher-student interactions, there will, still, be times when the teacher tells, advises, judges, directs. In other words, teachers' responses should reflect the most appropriate way of responding at that given time.

If, for example, a student asks for permission to go to the washroom, a direct response is a better alternative than a paraphrase. If, for example, a student wants direction to the library, a direct response is a better alternative than a paraphrase. If, for example, a teacher sees a student behaving badly, a direct response is likely to be more effective than a paraphrase. Choosing the most appropriate response for each situation is one more facet of polishing one's interactive skills repertoire.

CONCLUSION

The last words on this topic are reminders: the importance of remaining respectful, of being inviting instead of commanding, of being genuine, and, of course, watching for the effect of what has been said on the student. When all of that is "in play," there are no "wrong" responses. When the students know you are on their side, that you care, that you are taking the time to acknowledge who they are and what they think and what they believe, whatever response you make will have a positive frisson.

NOTE

1. Reprinted by permission of the Publisher. From Selma Wassermann, *Introduction to Case Method Teaching: A Guide to the Galaxy*. New York: Teachers College Press. Copyright © 1994 by Teachers College, Columbia University. All rights reserved.

Chapter 7

The Teacher and the Curriculum

The image of a teacher standing in front of a classroom "teaching the lesson" as the students sit, silently, absorbing the information, is one that is so familiar that it has become a cliché. And it is true that even today, in an age where information technology (IT) has infiltrated almost every corner of our lives, that image of "teaching" persists.

It is more than 100 years since John Dewey (1916) introduced the concept of a student-centered curriculum, where students could be more actively engaged on learning tasks, while the teacher acted as tutor, coach, and mentor; yet student-centered teaching has never displaced that original perspective despite the many attempts to introduce change over the years (Cuban, 1982).

To cite a few examples, the "Primary Organic Day" (Ashton-Warner, 1963), the "Integrated Primary Day" (Brown & Precious, 1968; Howes, 1974), "case method teaching" (Wassermann, 1994), and, of course, the dramatic results of the *Eight-Year Study* (Aiken, 1943) provided elementary and secondary teachers with not only well-constructed, research-based rationales for introducing student-centered programs but also suggestions for classroom strategies to implement these methodologies.

While the success of these programs has been well documented, they flourished briefly and faded, as teachers and classrooms retreated to more traditional methods.

However, as the song goes, "The times they are a-changing." While it may be too soon to predict a revolution in teaching methods, the increasing infiltration of IT into educational practice may mean that there is no longer any recourse to fall back on the "tried-and-true" ways of yore.

IT AND THE CURRICULUM

The resource teacher was working with a small group of Grade 3 students, introducing them to a new tablet application for improving reading skills. One boy zipped through the exercise, finished, and sat back, smirking. The teacher asked him, "How come, Waylon, you finished so quickly?"

Waylon said, without guile, "I been doin' this stuff since I was three years old."

IT is not going to go away any time soon. It has permeated our lives both for good and for not so good. It has eased itself into school activities in a variety of ways. In fact, there are now more than a dozen resource books for teachers who wish to integrate IT into the curriculum (e.g., Roblyer & Hughes, 2018; Wentworth, Earle & Connell, 2004).

The application of technology, throughout the grades, into language arts, mathematics, social studies, geography, science, business studies, and visual arts, initiated and supported by large IT companies like Microsoft, is already commonplace. In fact, Microsoft wants to "integrate hi tech into every subject area, every grade level." If this sounds like overreaching, consider this:

> Many, if not most, students these days have their own devices: smartphones, iPhones, laptops, tablets. Some schools now have the budgets to purchase such hardware, as well as textbooks, as complements to learning. Some schools are including IT courses as a required part of the standard curriculum. The workforce not only of the future but of today demands more and more a profound and deep acquaintance with technology, whether you are hired by Google, or Amazon, or as a counter person at MacDonald's.

It's not only the devices but what IT offers on them that is already making a significant difference in how curriculum is shaped and delivered. Google, the search engine that is so familiar that its name has become a verb (Did you Google it?), offers immediate access to a world wide web of information. Do you want to know the date of the Battle of Hastings? The names of the important generals of the American Revolution? The issues that were behind the call to arms for World War I? The number of the Executive Order that was responsible for imprisoning Japanese Americans during World War II? Julia Child's recipe for boeuf bourguignon?

Of course, one has to be especially careful about the honesty and correctness of what is found on the Internet. Students who use this most excellent resource should be cautioned about checking facts before making assumptions about the veracity of the information. There are several fact-checking sites that do this, for example, www.factcheck.org.

A teacher's role as information dispenser may very soon be relegated to the archives of educational history. Google and Wikipedia have taken over that role, doing it more quickly, with more easy access, and with more substance in what is included. For example, keying in Executive Order 1066 brings up Wikipedia, which offers a trove of information, identifying related sources, that are highlighted in their response to your request for information.

For example, in searching for Executive Order 1066, one can also be referred to the president who signed that order, what an Executive Order means, why the Japanese were singled out for this treatment and the Germans not, who was excluded from the order, where the internment camps were located, what the consequences were for the Japanese who were interned, and more. In many ways, Google and Wikipedia more often trump, in spades, what the teacher knows and is able to communicate.

As an additional factor, the student is able to access the information at his or her own rate, not at the rate in which it is being dispensed by the teacher. Students are in control of their pace of learning. Individual pacing and selective reviewing are important advantages afforded by the search engines.

It is not only information dispensing that the IT devices offer. Many of them provide entry into apps (applications) that teach certain skills, for example, in reading, math, science, and ESL for immigrants who need help with a new language or English speakers who want to learn a foreign language. There are apps designed for students with special needs, for students who need help with social skills, for "social and emotional" learning. All of this, too, is done in a way that each learner can pace himself or herself through the process of acquiring these skills.

The best of these apps is taught through the medium of games; they are designed not only to motivate students to want to learn but also to engage them so that attention is never lagging. Watch a six-year-old on his or her tablet and it's clear to see that no one has to insist that he or she pay attention. The apps are designed to attract and maintain attention. In fact, it's a tough job to pull a student away from the task.

Of course, there are better apps and those that are less good; the best ones are designed by those "in the know" about kids and about how to deliver the skills in a way that is developmentally appropriate and include the necessary facets of skill development in a particular subject area. Making good choices becomes a big part of the educator's job, whether it be the teacher or those in the administration who are making the IT purchases.

When it comes to more sophisticated and difficult subjects, like physics, calculus, economics, and so on, another advantage of these apps is that they allow not only for individual pacing but also for review, when a concept or skill is not fully understood. The learner can set his and her own pace and also review whatever needs to be restudied. And the learner need not be embarrassed by having to ask for a review. All of this is done under the individual student's control.

Familiarity with IT has become an important addition to school curriculum, both at the elementary and secondary school levels. In many school districts throughout Canada and the United States, students at the intermediate and high school levels are now required to take a "digital learning" course to acquaint them with the devices and some of the applications that would give them more informed access to the digital world.

A FEW EXAMPLES OF EXISTING SCHOOL PROGRAMS INCORPORATING IT

a. Qualicum Beach Elementary School (Vancouver Island)

The Qualicum School District (No. 69) is located mid-island, on Vancouver Island in westernmost British Columbia. It includes two "alternative" schools, eight elementary schools, and two secondary schools, enrolling approximately 5,000 students.

The Qualicum Beach Elementary School's STREAM program, which incorporates science, technology, robotics, engineering, and math, is an elective option for Grade 4–7 students wishing that kind of concentration in lieu of the "regular" curriculum. In this stream, students build and share video games of their own creation. They design websites and podcasts as well as other IT creations.

According to a teacher's report, "the students begin by writing a story and then developing the characters that are in the story, creating a backstory for these characters. And once they have fully fleshed out what the game was going to be, and explored it from different angles, they proceed to Scratch (scratch.mit.edu) a programming software. They code the game from scratch" (Kveton, 2017). According to the news report, the key aim of the program is to teach computational thinking, which, in part, teaches students to organize problems in such a way that computers can understand and help.

Taking learning goals and teaching them in a technology-based way is a big part of the STREAM program. "Students learn with new tools; they use gaming software instead of pen and paper."

When the teacher was asked what it was like to teach nine-year-olds to build video games, she said, "It's quite incredible. It helps me to see that the limit of what we can teach kids is unlimited. They are able to embrace new technology so quickly; they even teach me things I didn't know, which is really cool to see" (Kveton, 2017).

Maya, a Grade 4 student in the STREAM program at Qualicum Beach Elementary School, was interviewed and asked to give her views about the program in which she was enrolled:

What devices are used in your classroom?
> *Tablets, laptops, smartphones.*

Who provides them?
> *The school provides computers, iPads, iPhones for spheros (N.B. spheros are small balls with lights in them that you can control in many different ways with a mobile device from a phone or tablet) snowball microphones, headphones/microphones, headphone splitters.*

What are you constructing on your device now?
> *I'm doing a website. I just finished making a podcast about books, scratch.mit.edu programs, Google slide shows.*

I believe you do this IT work in small groups. How many kids in your group?
> *Sometimes we have groups of three or less, usually. Sometimes four.*

How are the groups chosen? That is, do you get to pick whom you work with? Or does the teacher assign groups?
> *Sometimes students pick their own groups. Sometimes the teacher uses a randomizer. (N.B. Randomizers are devices that allow for random selection; it could be a separate device, or it can be found on a computer.)*

When you begin to construct something on your device, what are the first things you do?
> *We first plan out the steps, to figure out what we are going to do.*

How do you figure out the best way to start?
> *We talk to each other. To the group members.*

How do you decide if what you have done is good? Or if it needs fixing?
> *We can show it to the teacher. Or we do a self-review.*

What happens when the work is finished? How do you share it with the others in the class?
> *Google Drive! allows sharing with other people. You can choose who to share it with and who can edit and who can just view it.*

This is a hard question. What important things do you learn from doing this work?
> *Sometimes I learn something new about the computer I'm working on that I'm using.*

What do you like best about your class?
> *Messing around in scratch.mit.edu and seeing what weird things I can do.*

What is obvious from Maya's responses is how much control students have over what they are doing and what they are learning. The ingredients of self-selection, self-pacing, and choice are under the aegis of the students. This is a giant step removed from the traditional classroom delivery of curriculum, where most, if not all, control is in the hands of the teacher.

b. Golden High School*

Golden High School is a large high school located just outside a major metropolitan area of Canada. The area is characterized by a high density of technology industry located in and around the city. The school has a population of 1,050 students and 68 staff members. The majority of students come from lower-middle to upper-middle-class families.

The school opened in September 1999 and was intentionally wired and designed to incorporate a focus on technology. Technology is integrated throughout the school rather than isolated in one given area. Computers are available in computer labs and in each classroom in the school. A wide range of software programs are available. All students at all grade levels are involved with technology throughout the curriculum. "Technology is used on a daily basis as a facilitative tool for learning and for various school activities." See, for example, https://www.oecd.org/innovation/research/2732912.pdf[1]

An example given in the school's website offers the following information about how IT is interwoven into the curriculum:

> "Two grade 10 students worked under the direction of the former vice-principal to create a web page that demonstrated an understanding of HTML, design components, graphic and content size limitations, and school/community needs. The students were matched with telementors at one of the school's partners, a major manufacturer of computers and peripherals. The students corresponded with their mentors twice per week, via e-mail, while designing the school's website.
>
> The mentors offered suggestions and helped troubleshoot the project. Student journals and all correspondence with the Telementors were reviewed with the vice principal. Students designed and completed a self-evaluation rubric at the end of the unit."

Some examples of how IT is integrated throughout the curriculum include the following:

- Assignments posted on the Web for students to select projects and resources listed with links
- Assignments e-mailed to teachers for assessment

- Chat room set up prior to exams so students can study collaboratively
- Math software supplement to curriculum
- Science simulations to supplement science lab experiments
- Dialogue with students in schools in other parts of the world comparing ideas and viewpoints
- Video and sound editing connected to live performances in the theater
- Marketing and computer classes
- Yearbook, newsletters, desktop publishing projects

c. Virtual Schools

There are, of courses, "virtual" and online schools located throughout the United States. According to the Molnar (2019) report, there are currently 501 full-time virtual schools, enrolling almost 300,000 students, located in 39 states. (These are full-time learning institutions, operated for profit by EMOs, that depend wholly on technology to deliver the curriculum.) The arguments have been made that these virtual schools can be tailored to individual students more effectively than curriculum in traditional classrooms. (The claims, however, have not been supported by research evidence.)

However, the promise of lower costs, primarily for instructional personnel and facilities, continues to make virtual schools financially appealing to both policymakers and for-profit providers (Molnar, 2019).

Virtual schools, however, are not addressed here, as they represent a different kind of education altogether, one in which teachers, at distance, play consulting, mentoring, and evaluative roles, rather than as classroom teachers and curriculum developers.

It should be noted that Minerva University, based in San Francisco, offers a four-year undergraduate program as well as a master's degree in science, in which all teaching is done online. "Though extensive research on the science of learning proves lectures to be ineffective, even top universities cling to this outdated instruction method. At Minerva, every class is a small seminar designed to keep you actively engaged, improving your grasp of practical knowledge, while deepening your understanding of specific subject matter." See, for example, https://www.minerva.kgi.edu/

WHAT CAN A TEACHER DO?

When the automobile replaced the horse and carriage as the most viable way of getting from place to place, doubters were quick to conclude that these "infernal machines" were merely a passing fancy. In those early years, refrigerators replaced ice-men who delivered large blocks of ice for "ice boxes," candles and gas lamps by electricity. None of these new technologies was greeted with open arms, and suspicion arose about whether they were safe.

Little by little, technology is replacing things that are more familiar to us. The jobs of switchboard operators, VCR repair workers, video store employees, typesetters, elevator operators, film projectionists have been wiped out in more recent years, replaced by technological innovation.

Encyclopedias and telephone directories have become icons of the past; road maps are replaced by GPS. The shopping mall is in decline as more people are using the convenience of online shopping. Large department stores are going bankrupt, while Jeff Bezos has become the richest man in America.

Will teachers find themselves in the job market as telementors in virtual schools replace them?

It depends.

From one writer's perspective, the prognosis is that if teachers continue to see themselves primarily as dispensers of information, they will most likely be replaced by more efficient, less costly technology found in virtual schools. But if teachers can envision themselves as high functioning professionals who are able to do the kind of teaching that the best devices and apps cannot do, they are more likely to continue to find their work not only complementary but essential.

How is this done?

There are likely more than a few ways for teachers to use teaching strategies and curriculum materials that engage students actively, collaboratively, and intelligently; that are relevant to the big ideas being studied; that call for student reflection on important issues; that promote student thinking; that develop a community of spirit among the learners; and that make school an exciting and meaningful place.

One of these is through the use of a "teaching for thinking" curriculum framework that incorporates all of these elements into a coherent whole. All elements serve to elevate students' thinking and build their intelligent habits of mind, deepen their understanding of the big ideas, and actively engage them with the material. Incorporated into all of these parts of the framework are the "thinking operations" (Raths, 1966), those higher-order mental processes that serve as the building blocks that are the foundation for all the parts in the framework. (The operations are highlighted in italics in the discussion below.)

In this curriculum framework, the learner begins to gather data by making observations (knowing). That step is followed by analyzing information (understanding) and leads to applying what is known to problem solving (knowing how).

Thus, in learning new material, students would work collaboratively, beginning with the gathering of data through their own *observations*.

Observations might be made, for example, through the viewing of a film or a DVD, examining an article, reading a story, examining the data in a graph or a table, observing the structure of a bridge, examining a list of metaphors, measuring the height of a "bounce" of different size balls, examining the voting record of a member of the U.S. Senate, examining original historical documents, studying the behavior of an animal, and learning the periodic table. Observations may be made on field trips to museums, factories, farms, studios, art galleries, newspaper offices, and so on.

The ways in which students can gather knowledge through observing are numerous, and with these examples as models, teachers may use their grade-level curriculum standards to devise their own curriculum tasks. Many curriculum tasks, in virtually every subject area, can be introduced through requesting that students gather data by making observations.

A second element of the framework requires students to "dig more deeply" into the information through the use of the operations of *comparing, classifying, looking for assumptions, suggesting hypotheses, summarizing,* and *interpreting data.* These operations call for different ways that students can deepen their understanding, by subjecting the information they have gathered to different kinds of analyses.

In this second step of the "teaching for thinking" framework, students can compare two historical documents, two stories by different authors, two celebrity figures, two different ways of solving a math problem, two different IT devices, two IT applications, two presidents, warm-blooded and cold-blooded animals, a president and a prime minister, two works of art, two pieces of music, and so forth.

They can classify historical documents, stories in a short story collection, prime ministers of England, African nations, animals used for human food, bodies of water, styles of clothing, and so forth.

They can look for assumptions in televised speeches of candidates for office, in newspaper *op ed* pieces or editorials, in advertisements, in global warming forecasts, in conclusions generated after a laboratory test, in conclusions made from graphed data, in data gathered from polls, and so forth.

They can suggest hypotheses to explain why some people need glasses, why some are allergic to certain foods, why some are more vulnerable to disease, why rents are more expensive in certain parts of town, why ball players earn more money than teachers, what makes some people more popular than others, why some people are short and some are tall, why some people hold racist views, why the moon causes tides to rise and fall, why our diets are so loaded with sugar, why some people are vulnerable to disinformation, why some people insist on holding a particular belief contrary to hard evidence, and so forth.

These are only a very few examples of how data coming from students' observations can be analyzed. In this framework, this stage in the process is part of "building understanding," and it is frequently aided and abetted in a class discussion called "debriefing." During debriefing, the teacher's use of higher-order questions and responses are used to sharpen students' awareness, insight, and understanding as students are called upon to respond with thoughtful, intelligent analysis of information.

Debriefing requires a teacher's skill in listening to and comprehending students' meanings; encapsulating their ideas in tightly woven paraphrasing; formulating questions that call for students' intelligent examination of key issues; orchestrating the discussion so that all students feel safe to volunteer their ideas, so that all students' ideas are respected; and keeping the discussion "on track" so that it does not go off course by students' introduction of personal anecdotes and unrelated issues.

In debriefing, teachers are required to suspend their need to tell students what they think. They must refrain from passing judgment on a student's ideas.

On other side of the coin, from the students' perspective, debriefing demands the best that students can give. No one is spared from doing his or her best thinking about the issues. As the semester unfolds, students learn the seriousness of the importance of reasoning from the data. The yield from rigorous examination of ideas in debriefing is manifest in students' responses over time. Habits of intelligent thinking grow.

The teacher's ability to conduct an effective debriefing, to enable students to bring sharper analysis to bear on the issues, and to work toward deeper insights is the *sine qua non* of artistry in teaching. Not even Siri—that virtual assistant from Apple, who uses voice queries and a natural language interface to answer questions, make recommendations, and perform actions by delegating requests to a set of Internet services—can replace the skills of a teacher in the process of debriefing. Debriefing is a consummate act of mining for gold in the educational process.

Any lived experience of students can be examined for deeper understanding using the skills and artistry of debriefing.

In the best of circumstances, debriefing is followed by providing students opportunities to apply what they know to practice. This stage of curriculum development involves the thinking operations of *problem solving, applying principles to new situations, decision making, designing projects, inventing,* and *creating*.

Students can apply what they know in designing an investigation to determine how they can tell that the moon affects tides, how a telephone survey can be used to gather data about preferences, how a campaign might be mounted to deal with littering in the school yard, how a campaign might be mounted to support recycling efforts in the school, how students might have an effective voice in addressing world problems, such as child labor, and how a project might be designed to demonstrate how the respiratory system works in humans or animals.

Once again, in this "knowing how" stage in the framework, the teacher's use of reflective responses and higher-order questions plays a major role in promoting students' knowing how.

The fourth part of the framework calls upon students to evaluate their work. Here, too, the teacher uses reflective responses and higher-order questions to put students' responses under further examination. What was good about their work? What would they like to have improved? Where does what they did need "fixing"? What kind of fixing is needed? What new understanding was acquired? What additional information is needed? And most important, what are the standards by which these assessments are being made?

These reflections that engage students in such self-scrutiny revisits what has been learned, puts students' work under their own critical eye, allows them to "own" what has been done, develops their strength and competence in self-assessment, and opens the door to further inquiry. This part of the framework uses the operations of *criticizing* and *evaluating* and puts students on the pathway toward becoming critical evaluators of their own work.[2]

A TEACHING FOR THINKING CURRICULUM FRAMEWORK

Part 1: Gathering knowledge through observing

Part 2: Furthering understanding through comparing, classifying, looking for assumptions, suggesting hypotheses, summarizing, interpreting data

Part 3: Applying knowledge through problem solving, designing projects and investigations, applying principles to new situations, making decisions, inventing, and creating

Part 4: Reflecting on action through evaluating and assessing

An important part of the above is the teacher's creation of a harmonious, caring, community in the classroom—the promotion of a group ethos where students learn to live together and work cooperatively. It is a given that IT devices may be part and parcel of any of the above, with the exception of the teacher's role in "debriefing" the students' work. That pivotal role belongs exclusively to the teacher.

These are not the only things that master teachers can do; there are others. But these are seen as essential ingredients in what teachers can do to make a difference to the quality of thinking and life of students in addition to and as complement to the technological advances that appear more and more in our lives. None of that can be surpassed by technology, no matter how sophisticated and compelling in design and format.

PUTTING THE TEACHING FOR THINKING CURRICULUM FRAMEWORK INTO PRACTICE

Brenda Price taught a Grade 6 class in a suburban community adjacent to a large west coast city. She was committed to the goals of promoting students' intelligent habits of mind and was about to design a curriculum plan that followed the teaching for thinking framework described above. She began by checking the state-mandated standards for her grade, knowing that her students might be tested at the end of the year on those standards. She was clear that the curriculum plan that called for students to exercise critical mindedness did not require a break with those standards.

She also wanted to incorporate some IT into the student's curriculum experience.

The standard she selected from the social studies state requirements was 6.18:

"Evaluate the impact of systems of colonial cultures on the indigenous peoples, such as termination, sovereignty, and treaties."[3]

She began by asking the students to work in teams of two, open their tablets or laptops, key in the URL: https://www.theatlantic.com/education/archive/2019/03/traumatic-legacy-indian-boarding-schools/584293/, and read the article about residential schools. (*Observing*) She wrote four questions on the whiteboard and asked them to team up with another team of two and discuss their responses to the questions. Then, working alone, they were to formulate their own written responses to them. They could do this on their laptops, tablets, or paper.

1. What, according to the article, do you see as some purposes of the residential schools for Native Americans? (*Observing*)
2. How, in your view, were children treated in these schools? (*Interpreting*)
3. Why do you suppose some parents were opposed to sending their children to the residential schools? (*Suggesting hypotheses*)
4. What, in your view, was the long-term impact of these schools on the children, the parents, and the Native American culture? (*Interpreting, evaluating*)

When the students had completed their assignment, she called the class together to "debrief" the curriculum task. A sample of the teacher-student discussion follows:

Teacher: You've all read the article and talked together about the questions I asked you to discuss. Let's start with Question 1. I'd like to hear your ideas about what you see as the purpose of the residential schools in the United States. Yes, Sean. You've had your hand up.

Sean: It's obvious to me that the purpose was to wipe out the Native culture and to assimilate the children into the dominant culture. I had no idea before. It was disgusting.

Teacher: You see one purpose was to destroy the Native culture and replace it with the Christian culture. The story about what happened to these children was repugnant to you. (*Paraphrases both the content and the feelings*)

Sean: How could they do that? How could the government do that to the Native peoples?

Teacher: You're outraged that a government could set a policy that would eradicate the culture of a group of people. (*Paraphrases*)

Sean: I could hardly believe it of my government. That they would do that.

Teacher: It seems hard to believe of your government. (*Paraphrases*)
 Why do you suppose they did it, then? (*Asks for hypotheses*)

Sean: I think it was to try to make the Indians like the rest of us. Maybe something about the Indians was threatening.

Teacher: The Indians posed a threat to the government? How did that become a reason to wipe the culture out? (*Paraphrases; asks for hypotheses*)

Sean: I don't know. Maybe it had something to do with those films we saw about how the Indians went on the warpath and tried to murder the settlers.

Teacher: Perhaps it had its roots in the fact that the government was concerned about what the Native populations could do. Especially when the pioneers were moving west and taking land that was formerly Native territory. (*Paraphrases; interprets*)

Sean: Yeah. I think so.

Teacher: Does anyone else want to add to what Sean has said? (*Invites others to respond*)

Margo: It didn't surprise me. From what I know about what happened then, about the way the Native peoples were treated, and how the government wanted to make sure the Indians didn't make any trouble.

Teacher: You see some other reasons for the government's stepping in and taking the children from their homes. (*Paraphrases*) What the article called "The Indian problem." (*Interprets*)

Margo: Yeah.

Teacher: So what, in your view, was the "Indian problem"? (*Asks for an interpretation of the term*)

Margo: I'm not sure. I'll let someone else answer.

Teacher: Thanks, Margo. (*Appreciates her response*) You want some more time to think about it. (*Interprets her reluctance to respond*) I understand these are powerful and worrisome ideas. (*Interprets the reason for lack of response*)
Jaime: You know, it's not unlike what the missionaries did when they went to other native cultures, like in Africa and Asia, and did some terrible things to the natives in order to get them to convert to Christianity.
Teacher: You see a relationship, Jaime, to what the missionaries did, as comparable to what the U.S. government did by establishing the residential schools. (*Paraphrases*)
Jaime: Yes, I do.
Teacher: Thanks for adding that idea, Jaime. I want to shift gears, now, and ask what you see as the impact of these schools on not only the children but on the parents and on the Native American cultures. (*Raises a challenging question by asking for an evaluation of what occurred*)

The discussion continues until the teacher has heard the students' ideas, and she is satisfied that she has brought the important ideas under discussion.

For the next stage in the inquiry into residential schools, the teacher will show the film *Bury My Heart at Wounded Knee* and ask them to do a Google search to examine other documents about residential schools, Native cultures, and the enforced move of natives to reservations. Fact checking the data from the Internet sources is an important part of their Internet searches.

This stage will be followed by asking the students to work in teams of two to interview a Native American of their own choosing to learn about that person's experiences as a child or as an ancestor of a child in a residential school and/or who lives on a reservation.

Further studies will involve investigations into the status of current selected Native cultures through readings, Internet searches, and field trips.

Finally, the area of inquiry will culminate in asking students to reflect, personally, on the overall of their experiences, to evaluate what they have done, and to write a summary of what meaning was taken from their work.

The "teaching for thinking" curriculum framework suggests a way to design curriculum experiences. Of course, the time allocated for progression from one stage to the next and to completion will understandably vary, depending on the developmental levels of the students and the teacher's sense of how much time should be allowed for each stage. Virtually any topic can be taught under this rubric. It is a given that students will be working on these tasks in cooperative learning groups, thereby aiding and learning from each other, an important ingredient in building community and unifying the group.

WHY DO THESE STUDENTS LOVE SCHOOL?

In 1999, Dorothy Fadiman made a documentary film called *Why Do These Kids Love School?*[4]

What leaps out of the frames of the film is the frisson of excitement the students reveal as they engage in their school activities. In all of the examples, there is emphasis on group collaboration, hands-on projects and investigations, and, in the overall, a high level of student engagement in the process of learning. The students exercise considerable control over what they are doing; the teachers are mentors, "guides on the side," supporters, encouragers, inspirers, and innovators. Respect for the students is palpable. Clearly these students love their schools, love what they are doing, and are eager to come to school to learn.

A Google search shows that not only do these schools exist today but they continue to thrive. None of them has retreated from their early mission of student-centered education.

When students love school; when they look forward to each school day; when they feel a sense of inclusion, of excitement in what they are doing, of knowing that they are respected and cared about, of having some control over what they do; when there is clear purposefulness to their learning tasks; and when there is a collaborative spirit and a sense of community in the classroom and in the school, the chances are better that such schools will survive and not be replaced by virtual education.

The curriculum framework proposed in this chapter is one way in which teachers may provide this kind of milieu, this kind of rich educational environment for students. It is not the only program that can work to the benefit of students, but this one, at least, may provide teachers with some ideas, some suggestions, some tools that may be used to put into practice a curriculum that brings out the best in students and makes a difference in their lives.

There are no guarantees, but it is a strong start.

NOTES

1. The PDF that describes Golden High School on this website came from OECD, the Organization for Economic Cooperation and Development, the international organization that sponsors and supports scientific and technological innovation. Although "Golden High School" could not be found in an Internet search, it has been assumed, given the data in the PDF, that the name is a pseudonym for an existing school in a suburb of a large city in Canada.

2. This material has been adapted, with permission: Reprinted by permission of the Publisher. Selma Wassermann, *Teaching for Thinking Today: Strategies, and*

Activities for the K-8 Classroom. New York: Teachers College Press. Copyright © 2009 by Teachers College, Columbia University. All rights reserved.

3. https://www.oregon.gov/ode/educatorresources/standards/socialsciences/Documents/Adopted%20Oregon%20K-12%20Social%20Sciences%20Standards%205.18.pdf.

4. The film captured innovative school programs like the one at Peninsula School in California, Graham and Parks School in Cambridge, Massachusetts, Central Park East Secondary School in New York City, Clara Barton Open School in Minneapolis, Clement Gregory McDonough City Magnet School, in Lowell, Massachusetts, Jefferson County Open School in Lakewood, Colorado, Central Park East II in New York City, and Davis Alternative Magnet School in Jackson, Mississippi.

*(https://en.wikipedia.org/wiki/Why_Do_These_Kids_Love_School%3F).

Chapter 8

Evaluation as a Tool for Improving Learning

"Madame Cheeeild," the teacher berated Julia Child, after her class at the Cordon Bleu School in Paris, "You will never be a cook."

Oh no! Not another task for teachers? As if attending to one's own emotional and physical health, learning to diagnose individual learning difficulties and addressing them with appropriate teaching strategies and materials, using teacher-student interactions that elevate students' intelligent habits of mind, creating a curriculum framework that engages students intellectually, and creating a harmonious and caring working environment are not enough. There is one more immensely important task that master teachers do:

Giving evaluative feedback to students that provides them with the understanding and the skills they need to advance their learning.

CREATING MORE EFFECTIVE ASSESSMENT TOOLS

Like the cliché of teaching as giving information, the cliché of evaluation is seen in the way a teacher "marks and grades" students' papers. That idea comes from repeated and deeply rooted in-school experiences in which teachers scan students' right and wrong answers on a written exercise, putting a large red X on the wrong ones, adding up the correct answers and errors, and placing a mark at the top of the page. This has as much to do with evaluation as MacDonald's has to haute cuisine.

If the essential purpose of evaluation is to shed light on where and how the learner is having difficulty and give feedback that not only points out that difficulty but also contributes to better understanding, the act of marking and grading does little to advance that purpose. Knowing what is "wrong" does not help to know what is right.

What's more, when marking and grading reveal a tsunami of wrong answers, such feedback inevitably undermines that student's confidence in his or her own abilities. In other words, not only does marking and grading *not* serve the purpose of advancing understanding, it has a negative effect of contributing to a student's loss of confidence in self. The ugly truth of marking and grading does not only not build understanding but its essential purpose is to rank students in a top-down hierarchy of where a student "sits" in relation to others in the class.

That such a system prevails in classroom practices is an anomaly; for more than a hundred years, researchers have brought to light the unsoundness of the measures used to assess students' work (Finkelstein, 1913). The unfairness of these measures, the errors, inaccuracies, their unreliability, and the variations in teachers' judgments have been long denounced, yet the system persists (Durm, 1993). It's hard to understand why so much value is put on numbers and letters that have such little meaning outside of the ways in which students are ranked.

Another, perhaps even more insidious consequence of these testing, marking, and grading systems is how they are used to evaluate teachers. While evaluating teachers by students' scores on these unreliable tests is one further step in promoting egregious errors in measurement to fallacious ends, such a system persists as well. Ravitch (2020), a strong advocate for school improvement, has made a vigorous stand against such a pernicious system; "it is not only unscientific, but given the many aspects of students' lives over which teachers have no control, grossly unfair."

Perhaps it's because we tend to love numbers; they seem to give us grounding, a sense of certainty in a world in which so much is in flux. Be that as it may, marks and grades are counterproductive in the advancement of student learning.

What is helpful is a teacher's ability to diagnose where and how the student is having difficulty, zero in on the problem or problems, provide feedback that addresses the difficulty and points to what the student needs to do to take the next steps in learning.

Those teaching acts begin with the kinds of assessment instruments that may be used to make such diagnoses. In other words, a "test" or written exercise that asks only for single correct answers may be easy to mark and grade, but it is not going to reveal a student's understanding of the big ideas of what is being studied. Such an instrument may also ask for irrelevant or inconsequential pieces of information (e.g., In what year did Shakespeare graduate from high school?) that shed no light on "what's important."

Developing an evaluative instrument that would, in fact, give students a chance to show what they know and what they understand, reflecting what has been taught and supposedly learned, is the starting point. The teacher decides as to what's important for the students to know, and what kind of assessment tool best reveals that understanding.

A teacher using the curriculum framework presented in chapter 9, where the activities flow from the "higher-order thinking operations," may choose to create assessment instruments that are designed to reveal how the student is observing and analyzing the information from the curriculum activity. With such tools, the teacher may have a "better handle" on assessing the quality of thinking as well as the comprehension of the big ideas.

For example, in chapter 9, in the example given for the learning standard for Grade 6 social studies, that is, "Evaluate the impact of systems of colonial cultures on the indigenous peoples, such as termination, sovereignty, and treaties," the teacher began the students' inquiries with a study of the article about residential schools that students had read in teams of two. She asked them to pair up with another team of two to discuss the questions she had posed for them on the whiteboard. The questions asked for their observations and their analyses of the material.

Once the students had a chance to read, reflect, and discuss the questions, the teacher could create an assessment tool that would include one or more of the teacher's whiteboard questions. Such a test would help her determine the extent to which the students had grasped the important issues behind the creation of the residential schools, the treatment of the children in the schools, and the long-term impact on the children and parents of this kind of education and on the Native cultures.

Student responses to these questions would reveal not only their understanding of the big ideas, the critical issues but also how they processed the information they read in the article. It would also shed light on how the students were grappling with the big ideas behind the state-mandated standard about colonialism and its effects on original cultures. It would give the teacher important information about how the students were "making meaning" of what they had read and discussed.

Of course, reading, evaluating, and giving feedback to all students about their work on such assessment tools will, undoubtedly, take more time than simply eyeballing the list of what is wrong and what is correct on a test that simply adds up right and wrong answers. There's no mistake about that. But teachers who have shifted from right and wrong assessment exercises have claimed that reading students' papers are much more interesting, and enlightening, and the educational benefits more valuable, than marking and grading.

Like most things, it is the teacher who ultimately decides what is more important in his or her view for the benefit of student learning. It has been noted that those teachers who have chosen these more productive and more valuable assessment tools have not looked back.

DIAGNOSING STUDENTS' DIFFICULTIES

The first step in examining students' papers is to get an overall sense of what the student is saying. This should be done before any feedback is given, to ensure that the teacher has a full comprehension of the student's overall response. A second reading should focus on where the student went beyond the data in making observations, made unwarranted assumptions, missed important issues, made errors in judgment, made factual errors, made attributions, and made personal judgments that were unwarranted. Spelling and errors of grammar might also be noted.

The second step is for the teacher to zero in on those issues. In doing so, two principles should obtain:

1. There is no "truth" in evaluating students' work. The judgments lie in the eye of the beholder. How the teacher perceives the students' responses and makes the determination of whether those responses meet the evaluative criteria is the teacher's opinion. Not the truth.
2. The teacher need not comment on or evaluate everything the student has written. This would not only make the task too unwieldy for the teacher. It would also give the student more than he or she can handle.

The third step is to determine what the teacher believes needs to be brought to the student's attention. That is, pointing out where the important problems are seen.

The fourth is to find the best ways to write feedback that addresses the important issues in a way that is respectful and enabling and suggests what the student might do to emend the work.

An example of the way the steps are executed should make the principles clearer:

Using the example from chapter 7 about residential schools, the teacher has created the following "test" questions for her Grade 6 class as part of a summary assessment of their understandings from their unit on colonialism. What guides her formulation of those questions is her desire to discover how the students have understood the important ideas.

1. What have you observed about the purposes of the residential schools for Native Americans?
2. What do you see as the consequences of that imposed schooling on Native culture, on family, on language, on the self-esteem of the students?
3. In your view, was it wrong for the U.S. government to attempt to "civilize" Native Americans by sending them to residential schools? What is your argument for and against that policy?

Mai Lee's response:

1. *They wanted to wipe out the Indian culture. They wanted to make the Indians more like the white people.*
2. *The schools took children away from their parents and taught them the ways and the culture of the white peoples. A lot of children suffered from bad treatment. They were not allowed to speak in their own language. They were made to feel ashamed for what they were. That was what happened to them.*
3. *It was a bad thing to do. I think a government should not try to wipe out a culture. It's wrong for one group of people to think they are better than another group. I know that was true for Asians who came to America long ago too. It's prejudice I think.*

There are several pathways that her teacher can take to illuminate the strengths and areas that need further consideration on Mai Lee's paper. None of the pathways is "the right way." The teacher's choice reflects what she knows about the student, about the student's past history in her classroom work, and, of course, the information the student has given about the residential schools, their underlying mission, and the impact of colonial cultures on indigenous peoples. In other words: how has the student used the higher-order operations to make insightful meaning of what has been read and discussed?

These issues are what guides the teacher's feedback: Has the student made accurate and fair observations? Made unwarranted assumptions? Gone beyond the data? Has the student grasped the important ideas behind what the government did in creating residential schools? Does the student see broader issues that extend from such government initiatives?

GIVING EVALUATIVE FEEDBACK

Two principles guide the teacher's feedback to the students. One is zeroing in on what the student has misunderstood or where the student has gone far beyond the data. The other is pointing to the steps the student might take in furthering understanding. These comments should both reflect that they are the teacher's judgments and indicate that they are not the truth. They do not need to exclude the teacher's positive judgment about the overall quality of the work, should that be the case. No student is averse to getting feedback that suggests that his or her work has been, in the teacher's judgment, of notable quality.

Writing feedback on a student's written, pencil-and-paper assignment is more easily done in pencil, which allows for the teacher to erase any word or statement that, upon reflection, may seem unwarranted, unclear, or hurtful. If the student's work has been done on a computer, editing one's comments is easy.

Teacher's feedback on Mai Lee's paper:

Hi Mai Lee. I was impressed with your thoughtful analysis in your responses to each of the questions. I can see that what was done in the residential schools has deep meaning for you. I have a few comments to make on each question. Perhaps you can think about my comments and see how you might extend your thinking about the issues.

1. *In question #1, you write that the government wanted to wipe out the Indian culture and make the Indians more like the white people. That seems to me to represent the main idea behind the establishment of the residential schools. Can you think about why the whites thought themselves as superior to the Indians? Any ideas about that?*
2. *You mention several things that happened to the Indian children at the residential schools, including the ways in which the children were abused. I wonder how these school experiences shaped their later lives. Do you have any further ideas about that?*
3. *In your third answer, you suggest that a government should not try to influence the culture of a different group of peoples. Can you give some examples how the U.S. government did this in other countries? And how other countries did that as well?*

In this teacher's response to Mai Lee, she first appreciates her answers, pointing out the thoughtfulness shown in her responses. The teacher also asks extending questions for each of the student's answers, opening up a broader line of inquiry about colonialism and its effects on native populations.

There is a legion of possible responses to Mai Lee's paper. How the teacher responds will reflect that teacher's overall view of what's important to highlight and how the teacher wants to encourage the student to think more about the big ideas underlying the social studies "standard." Obviously much more can be discussed, read, and examined about the role of colonialism, manifest in one example of the residential schools, both for the occupying country and for the occupied. And once again, it lies in the teacher's judgment about how far and how deeply to explore the issues and when to cut and run and move on to the next topic.

In the final analysis, the teacher makes these decisions. And while it's agreed that virtually any topic or standards goal can be exploited to the ends of time, certain limits must be set, since the time allocations for what is taught and learned in any grade have clear boundaries. One can't have it all, but one can have the best that we can make of it.

It should also be noted that teachers' evaluative feedback need not only be on tests. Such feedback can be helpful on any written assignment, including homework.

STUDENTS' SELF-EVALUATIONS

One of the more important skills that students can learn is to make their own self-assessments of their work. Given that more mature, more independent adults have their locus of evaluation within themselves, and do not have to rely on any outside authority to tell them if what they have done is "good," learning to become more self-aware of one's strengths and areas of needed improvement seems an important tool for students to develop. It is, unfortunately, one that is sadly neglected in their school experiences.

This is not to say that all of their work should be self-evaluated, but surely students can do more of this—as much as the teacher sees as viable in the course of a term or a semester's work. Of course, some assignments may not lend themselves to self-assessment, and once again it is the teacher's choice with respect to which ones can and should be subject to the student's self-scrutiny.

The more students gain the power and the skill to evaluate themselves, the more teachers have given them the tools for becoming more mature and more self-sufficient adults.

In the first steps toward students becoming more thoughtful, introspective, and insightful self-evaluators, teachers may present them with some "keys" to that self-understanding, keys that target what the student can assess. These guidelines can be omitted once students have moved ahead in the acquisition of self-evaluation skills. Using once again Mai Lee's answer sheet, and putting her in the position of examining her own work, the teacher might ask her to do the following self-assessment:

1. How did you go about locating the information you needed for your responses?
2. How did your discussions with your partner and with the other team help you to find better responses to the questions?
3. What parts of the questions did you find more difficult? How did you manage those difficulties?
4. On which questions did you think you might have made more complete responses?
5. How did this work help you to understand the role of colonialism as it was revealed in the establishment of the residential schools?

A student's work on self-evaluation does not replace the teacher's assessment; the two can be parts of the whole of feedback on students' work, each with its own purpose and goals. But the importance of students' growth in becoming self-assessors, at any grade level, cannot be overestimated.

While students may not find their way to these self-assessments an easy road, they do learn to do this better with experience over time. And after time, it becomes a natural act. Implicit in the development of these students' skills is the teacher's willingness to cede a part of his or her prerogatives in evaluating students' work, recognizing that such skill development is a big part of student empowerment.

REPORTING TO PARENTS

When teachers have taken the trouble to use evaluative feedback on students' assignments and tests, they will find that they have amassed an abundant store of information about that student and that student's work. This is a valuable data source when teachers meet parents for parent-teacher conferences and/or in writing formative or summative reports home.

Most parents want to know how well their son or daughter is doing. Many parents are eager to help, when called on to play a role in furthering their son or daughter's knowledge base. And many of them will happily cooperate with a teacher to that effect. Giving parents good information about a student's competence, their strengths, their areas of needed improvement will unite them in a partnership in which the child is the beneficiary.

On the other side of the coin, no parent wants to hear that their son or daughter is doing poorly or failing or showing demonstrable signs of poor work. That is why reporting to parents should be sensitive to parental needs and concerns, elevating the positive and being caring and respectful in identifying where further help is needed.

When a teacher meets with parents, it is helpful to have samples of the student's work to present, pointing to specific evidence of what the student has done, how it has been done (successfully or not), and where further work is needed. The samples of work support what the teacher is saying, making the judgments concrete. It is also helpful for teachers to have prepared, in advance, what he or she is going to say to the parent. This is especially true for secondary school teachers who have, perhaps, dozens of students about whom they are reporting to parents.

In many schools, students, even at the primary grade level, are now included in teacher-parent conferences, and this not only has proven to be additive but also puts the onus on the student to be a faithful and insightful judge of his or her own work. Once again, the student should be given some guidelines that would pave the way for a smooth and helpful discussion about the student's work. The student may also choose which work he or she would like to show the parent and which activities, tasks, in-school experiences should be discussed.

What is less than valuable in reporting to parents is the use of "educational jargon," such as "he is working up to his potential," and descriptors that have little meaning or are subject to incorrect interpretations. To be specific, to back up judgments with examples, to emphasize the positive, to separate the judgment about the work from a judgment about the student—all serve to make the reports to parents clear, in a realm in which much is at stake for parents as well as students. If not the teacher's most difficult and complex task, it is surely one of the most fraught with personal and practical dimensions.

CONCLUSION

If there are principles that can be drawn from the work that teachers do in evaluating students' assignments and tests, these seem to be the more relevant:

- Remember that all evaluation is subjective and not truth. Judgments lie in the eye of the beholder and making that explicit is both fair and honest. Or as the elder in a Cree tribe commented: it depends on where you sit on the medicine wheel.
- No one, not the young, nor the adult, is immune to the hurtful negative judgments made by others. Tempering judgments about students with a care to protect their fragile egos should be uppermost in the minds of teachers as they issue their evaluative judgments. In other words, in evaluating students' work, first do no harm.
- Use assessment tools that are appropriate to the big ideas of the topics that are being studied. Single correct answer tests are a poor example of determining a student's understanding of "what's important."
- In diagnosing those areas where students' need help or where they have shown particular strengths, be specific. Words like "good" or "needs improvement" do little to point to how the work meets or fails to meet the standards.
- Provide feedback that incorporates what the student might do to further his or her thinking or skill development. Specific suggestions are more helpful than generalizations.
- In order to protect oneself from exhaustion in assessing students' work, teachers might remember that it is not critical to evaluate every piece of

work a student does. Nowhere is it writ that giving evaluative feedback should take precedence on every other task a teacher must face in his or her teaching day.

It is not within a teacher's power to make evaluation painless for themselves and for their students, but it is possible to reduce the amount of unnecessary pain and increase its usefulness to both students and parents.

Chapter 9

Teaching as a Courageous Activity

A new teacher, she wanted to individualize her reading program because she no longer saw that teaching reading in three ability-related groups was a viable option. There were children in her Grade 3 class who no longer could be accommodated in that kind of grouping. Teaching to the "middle" did not serve the children at either ends of the groups. Uncertain about making such a change from the school's standard practices, she went to her principal to put the case forward.

The principal listened, smiled sweetly, and offered: "Miss Carlin, I'm sorry. We don't do experimental programs here at Abbey Lane. We only use the tried and proven method."

Not every administrator wants to keep a choke hold on what teachers do in their classrooms. Not every board of education issues rules and regulations that stifle a teacher's use of new and innovative methods. In fact, in more than a few cases, administrators and school boards welcome innovation by providing professional-day workshops to encourage teachers to embrace new and more effective teaching strategies.

But what if a teacher sees the need to make a major change in the way curriculum is delivered, in the teaching strategies used to deliver that curriculum, and in the ways in which students are to be evaluated and faces constraints from an administrator, a school board, or fellow teachers? What options are open, so that his or her classroom practices are in accord with what that teacher believes is right and good for the students?

Chapter 9
THE CLOSED CLASSROOM DOOR

It has been noted that teachers play a solitary role in what they do, unlike other professions, where collaboration and associations with peers form a major part of their professional activities. Teachers work alone, in their own habitats, with doors closed to the observations and judgments of others. That is not to say that their work is not, in the long term, assessed by their supervisors or inspectors. That is not to say that parents don't play a role in making judgments about what a teacher does, in the event of their own child having difficulty.

But on a day-to-day basis, what teachers do in their isolated units of activity is of their own making, of their own choice. That closed door enables large degrees of freedom, to choose to stay close to the "tried-and-true" methods dictated by fiat or to use teaching practices that are in closer accord with the teacher's beliefs about what is best for the students in his or her domain. While there are downsides to the absence of collegiality in working in one's profession, there are definitely upsides to the privacy afforded to teachers in making choices of what they do and how they practice teaching.

Yes, it takes a certain amount of courage, especially for new teachers, to take the risks of swimming against the tide, of using teaching strategies that veer away from more traditional in-school practice. Yes, it takes courage to behave according to one's deeply held beliefs about the best teaching practices for one's students. And in making those decisions about whether to conform or to innovate, the teacher decides: What's important, for the students and for me as a growing professional?

The pathway that takes a person from conforming to more traditional practice is not smooth. In fact, history has shown that those men and women who have dared to be different have paid some prices before what they have advocated has been accepted and later, widely embraced. Ludwig Semmelweiss (1818–1856), who was the first to identify germs as the source of childbed fever that killed many women after childbirth, was driven out of the medical profession by colleagues who ridiculed his insistence that doctors wash their hands before surgery.

When the Wright Brothers built their first airplane in 1903, they too were condemned. "If God wanted man to fly, he would have given him wings." As were electric light bulbs ("a conspicuous failure"), Tesla's alternating current ("fooling around with alternating current is a waste of time"), telephones ("hardly more than a toy"), television ("a commercial and financial impossibility"), and automobiles ("the horseless carriage is a luxury for the wealthy and will never come into as common use as the bicycle").

And more recently: spacecraft ("a rocket will never be able to leave the Earth's atmosphere"), personal computers ("there's no reason anyone would want a computer in their home"), online shopping ("remote shopping, while feasible, will flop, because women like to get out of the house, like to handle merchandise, like to be able to change their minds"), and cell phones ("cellular phones will absolutely *not* replace local wire systems"). The list of innovations that were originally condemned that became essential features of modern life is legion.

That is not to say that a teacher's innovative classroom methods will become the next rage in educational practice. That is not to say that every innovation a teacher makes is sound or wise or effective for student learning. But that is also not to say that a teacher should not make the judgment calls about how best to serve and teach the students in his or her care. For if a teacher does not know the why and how changes should be introduced and used, who, outside of that classroom, is wiser, more informed, more skilled at directing the course of teaching practice for a particular group of students?

TEACHERS WHO DARED

It was her first year of teaching, having come from a teacher education program that advocated child-centered practices and gave her opportunities to hone her skills as a curriculum developer and practitioner of teaching for thinking classroom interactions. She accepted a Grade 3 position in a small town with a burgeoning population, in a school so recently built that it still smelled of fresh paint.

She began by doing all the things she had learned: orienting the children to her methods, outlining classroom procedures, enlisting the cooperation of parents, and developing curriculum experiences that engaged the children in hands-on problem-solving activities, followed by group discussions that probed their ideas and encouraged further examination of issues. Her respect for the children, her willingness to listen to them, her attention to their individual needs, and her thoughtfulness in what she did and what she said quickly won her students' admiration and regard.

Late in the spring, when the class had long become acclimated to her methods and had earned a large measure of independence, she was scheduled to be "observed" by her principal, who was to give a report on her work to the officials in the higher administration, to determine whether she was meeting their standards of teaching performance. Having faith in what she had accomplished and in how the students had progressed, she prepared nothing special other than what was on schedule for that morning.

The students were working in groups of three to four, engaged in science investigations examining simple machines. She had prepared a variety of easy-to-obtain simple machines, such as kitchen scales, scissors, staplers, can openers, garlic press, rotary eggbeater, timer, pulley, wheels of all sizes, wedges, screws, and screwdriver, and the students were examining the machines and making observations about how they worked and how they were used. She had asked them to make some notes about their observations to discuss in the large group debriefing of the activity.

During the hands-on group activity, she went around the classroom, making herself available to answer questions, to raise questions, to reassure a child who was having difficulty, and, of course, making a mental note of students who were having difficulty with the task. It was during this group activity that the principal came in to observe her. He went quietly to the rear of the room, sat on a visitor's chair, and watched the children at work and the teacher's one-on-one interactions. The room was abuzz with the productive noise of children as serious scientific investigators.

He sat there for perhaps twenty minutes or more, and then got up, walked over to her, and whispered in her ear, "I'll come back when you're teaching."

She was crushed.

In an after-school conference, the teacher, and the principal sat and discussed what she had been doing, the purpose of the activity, the progress the students had made. He listened quietly to her report and then told her that all of that was fine—except. She had to be prepared for her class to succeed on the standardized tests to be administered at the end of the school year. Her job was on the line. To keep her job for a second year, her students had to do well on the test.

A new teacher is vulnerable. She didn't have tenure to protect her. She had no mentor in the school to whom she could turn for advice or guidance. It was all down to her: What she believed, what she thought was best for her students, and how she admired how far they had come in learning not only skills but concepts. She was proud of the way they had become more thoughtful, more ready to think, more inquiry oriented. After several sleepless nights, she knew that she could only continue to teach the way she believed best for her students' growth and development.

The final result came in the children's performance on the standardized tests. The principal called her in to tell her the news. He was surprised but happy to tell her that her students had done as well, if not better than the Grade 3 students across the hall from her. Her continuation at the school for the following year was assured.

He had been teaching Grade 11 social studies in a suburban high school for at least a dozen years, known throughout the school by teachers and students as tough, demanding, and conservative in his thinking and teaching methods. He described himself as "to the right of Attila the Hun." In spite of that, he volunteered to participate in a two-year professional development outreach program to develop his skills as a case method teacher.

The professional development program was initiated by the assistant principal, with the blessing of the higher administration of the district. It was to involve the entire group of social studies teachers at the school. After three sessions of after-school workshops, twenty of the teachers withdrew; they wanted no part of changing their teaching methods to embrace a methodology that they believed would not ensure the students' passing the Grade 11 provincial social studies exams.

Joe was one of the three social studies teachers who chose to remain, along with several others from different subject areas. He never retreated from the professional demands of the workshops, spending long after-school hours writing cases, honing his teacher-student interaction skills in debriefing cases, and developing alternate assessment tools that were more compatible with case teaching methodology.

Despite the taunts of his colleagues and despite listening to their worries that his students would never pass the provincial exam, he persevered, bolstered by his students' responses to the sea change in his style, his attitude toward them, his granting them more degrees of freedom. More and more he was encouraged by their sophisticated responses to the higher-order questions he posed, by their palpable interest in the work, and by their consistent and eager attention in class. The responses of his students were more than sufficient to maintain his commitment in the face of collegial derision.

His students' scores on the Grade 11 provincial exam in June were more than adequate demonstration that the work he had done was successful. As a final piece of evidence of their interest, enthusiasm, and achievements, students completed projects that were examples of some of their important learning gains. There were videos, photo-displays, exhibits, recorded interviews, models—which he put on display in the classroom. A few of his colleagues caught a glimpse of the displays and said, "Our students are not capable of doing such sophisticated work."

She was a veteran teacher, with a solid reputation among parents, who saw her as dedicated and highly committed to the success of her Grade 1 students. Developing their reading and literacy skills was among her primary teaching goals, and she worked diligently to assure that by the end of the school year, most, if not all, of her students could read at the Grade 1 level and write simple words and sentences.

Her teaching took a major turn when she read Sylvia Ashton-Warner's book *Teacher* (1963); it was as if a light had been turned on in her head, and she puzzled over how different an approach was being advocated in this work and why these new methods had such resonance for her.

She took her first steps by meeting with her principal, who told her that while he was not opposed to her trying out these new methods, he was far from certain she would be able to attain the same kinds of success she had been having with her more traditional approaches. In fact, he wondered what was motivating her to make such a change.

She was not certain herself, but she did know that it was important for her to try. Somewhere within her she believed that this was a better way to teach children to read, tapping their inner worlds and bringing forth from them the words that were most important in their lives.

Like most of her other classroom work, she developed a clear plan of what she would do and how she would do it. She began by orienting the children, telling them what she was going to do and how she was going to do it, and giving them clear instructions as to what her expectations were for them. Feeling still uncertain about her competence to do this, she shut her classroom door, so that if there were going to be some downsides, she didn't want to have that exposed to any one passing down the hallway.

The children were told they could choose their books from the library shelf in the classroom and they were to team up in pairs and read to each other while she was having conferences with individuals, taking their "key vocabulary." On the whiteboard she listed the names of the six children with whom she was going to have conference that morning.

Tammie was the first to come to sit with her. Using the kinds of questions and responses she had read about in the text, she queried Tammie and found that her first key word was Jason, her older brother. There was obvious tension in that sibling relationship, and Tammie was the first to admit that Jason took her toys, provoked her, and was a "big pest."

The teacher wrote J-a-s-o-n on the cut-out piece of paper she had prepared for the key words and held Tammie's hand has she guided it over the letters, speaking the letters and indicating their sounds. At the end of the conference, she told Tammie to take her word and show it and read it to some of her friends in the classroom.

She followed similar methods with the other five children who had been slated for conferences with her that morning. During the time she had been conferencing with the children, there was no uproar in the class; the children, by and large, seemed happy and productively engaged with reading to each other. The children who had received their key words seemed delighted at the experience of having the teacher to themselves, in a private tutorial.

At the end of the morning, she was pleased with what appeared to be the first sign of success of her new trial. When the lunch bell rang and the children lined up at the door, Rudy sat at his desk weeping. She went over to him, sat down next to him, and asked him to tell her what was wrong.

He sobbed as if his heart was breaking. "You never took my word. I have no word to take home."

There are many stories in the Naked City of educational practice, and these are only a few of them. When teachers close their doors and take some giant steps away from more traditional practices, it is the students themselves that are the ones who provide the evidence that what has been done is beyond successful—not only in standardized measures but in what they know, what they feel, what they believe they have accomplished. The students are the "tell."

It is far easier for teachers to stay with the "tried-and-true" of traditional practice, but if that adage were to be closely examined, there's nothing true about tradition. It's just tradition. Growth comes from innovation, from taking steps beyond the norms into uncharted territory.

And yes, that is an act of courage.

Chapter 10

What's the Payoff?

He was complaining to his practicum supervisor about the trials and tribulations facing him, a student teacher, as he attempted to negotiate the many and varied performance tasks required of him each teaching day. "Teaching is hard," he moaned. "I don't know if I have the resources to commit to this kind of drain of my energies each and every day of a teaching life."

"Well," she replied with cheek, "if you wanted an easier profession, you could try neurosurgery."

Making a commitment to a teaching life is not for every person. It is true that those who are not "in the know" believe it to be a walk in the park. Leave for home at 3:00? Two-week holidays for Christmas and Easter? A two-month paid vacation in the summer? What could be sweeter than that? Yet, as every teacher knows, from intimate experience, leaving school at 3:00 means taking a load of students' papers home to read and evaluate; making phone calls to parents about a student in trouble; outlining plans for the following day, for the rest of the week; and designing appropriate activities for students who need special help. Why do it?

You have to love it. Love the experience of working with students, no matter what age. Love the creative act of designing curriculum that is singularly appropriate for individual learners and creating a classroom ethos that is engaging, lively, humane, caring. You have to love the exhilaration felt when there is tangible evidence of success in the way a student perceives a task, in the way independence grows, in the way students emerge from their cloistered selves and reach out to others with care and concern.

You have to love the rhythm of a dynamic teacher-student discussion when you see how students have become more thoughtful inquirers. You have to love the feeling that such evidence shows that your work has had intense and profound meaning in the lives of others.

Teachers are in the "people-growing" business. You have to love knowing that and being a part of the process. That is one payoff. But it's not for everybody.

WHAT'S IN IT FOR ME?

It's surely not the salary. If one counted all the in-school and after-school hours that teachers work at their jobs, it would probably compute to less than the minimum wage per hour for sweeping floors at Burger King.

It's not the physical working conditions. Some schools are so old that windows, which have been painted over so many times, no longer open in the heat of late June, and the staff rooms are either too hot or too cold and certainly not equipped with any comfortable furnishings.

Bells ring and buzzers and intercoms intrude when an important discussion is taking place. Teaching materials are in short supply; sometimes there are not enough textbooks for every student. Copy paper, duplicating resources, and art supplies are limited, and by the end of the school year, the supplies have dried up altogether. "Special" teachers for art, music, and physical education are the first ones cut when the budget is reduced. There is a long queue for students who need emotional help from a psychologist or school counsellor.

School boards, with little knowledge of what makes for effective teaching, dictate rules about time allocations, curriculum standards, report cards, and, in some cases, teaching methods. In some districts, "inspectors" come to observe and make hasty judgments without appreciating the full picture. In terms of payoffs, there is not much as far as physical or financial incentives go.

So, what is the payoff for teachers to stick it out, to work hard at trying to make a positive difference in the lives of their students, to become masters at their craft? You have to love the idea that you can do that; you have to love the sight of students who are advancing to places they themselves never believed possible. You have to love the idea that you are the one responsible for that growth, that change, that development.

And then, there are the sweet notes, letters, e-mails, and small gifts that come, once the class has passed into a teacher's memoirs, many from former students, some of them now adults with professional lives of their own, some from parents who recognize that what a teacher has done has had profound impact. For example:

> *If it wasn't for you, I wouldn't be a teacher today.*
>
> *You were more than my teacher. You were my mentor, my advisor, my confidant. I'll never forget you.*

You sit on my shoulder when I teach. Your teaching continues to teach me as I teach my students.

Each student contributed a dollar. We parents made this corsage of dollar bills for you for Christmas to show how much we all appreciate you and what you are doing.

If it weren't for the work we did in your class, I would not be able to stand in front of a group of professionals and give them a speech. You helped me to get confidence in myself and grow in my independence.

I was almost a delinquent! You showed me love and gave me a reason to become what I am today.

I was just granted tenure in my college. I would never have made it if it hadn't been for your confidence in me, your help, your support.

You showed me what education is all about and everything I have done since in education has been centered around making school a better place for kids.

You helped me become a better person.

Tracy has loved you so much. She has looked forward to every day of school with eagerness and pleasure. She has grown enormously in terms of human and emotional development. Thank you for always leaving her fragile dignity intact and for your many unmistakable displays of true love, not only toward her but toward the others in the class.

When I first had a reading conference with her I was unsure of myself and I really don't like to read, especially out loud, but she made most of that disappear because she is such a kind and wonderful person that she won my confidence. She makes me feel at ease. When I grow up I would like to be a person like her.

When I needed someone to believe in me and to give me a little extra attention and love, you were there.

Because of the wonderful inspiration you have been to me, I'll remain always and ever a very grateful student.

Many teachers who remain in the profession have their own collection of "valentines" from former students who reach out to let them know that their teaching has made a difference in their lives. But that is not why we teachers commit to the tasks that are often daunting, more often impossible, and, despite all our hard work, with few immediate signs of success. We do it for the thrill of being a part of a life-giving process that few other professions can match.

One of the more compelling pieces of evidence of a teacher's pride in a student's growth and development is seen in the end scenes of the film *The Kings Speech*. King George VI, who took the throne after the abdication of his brother, in 1937, was a lifelong stutterer. After many experiences with teachers who tried, unsuccessfully, to help him in the past, he was referred to

Lionel Logue, who had had long experience working with severely speech-impaired veterans of World War I.

Logue, using methods that were, in that time, unusual and innovative, allowed his "student" to find his own voice and helped him to overcome some of his fears. Little by little the future king became more confident and more secure in speaking, but even so, never fully polished.

At the outbreak of World War II, the King had to make a radio broadcast to all of his people, both at home and abroad, announcing the onset of the war, and ensuring them of his support for them. With Logue at his side, George, although terrified, read his speech with unfaltering success. The pride and the sense of satisfaction seen in the face of his teacher is manifest of what teachers everywhere know and feel as they take pride of accomplishment in the gains of their students—the teachers who have made a difference.

In the book *An Apple for My Teacher* (Rubin, 1987), the author collected a dozen essays from prominent writers who tell about how a single teacher has made a significant difference to their lives. "Whatever was taught, there was something about them that made the future author decide that the literary life, e.g., ideas, knowing things, putting words together on paper, was a dignified and worthwhile activity, meriting honor and respect" (Rubin, 1987). An entire book of essays is dedicated to the teachers who "lit the fires" that enabled them become the writers they are today.

This is what master teachers do. Lives are changed and shaped because of them. Fragile students grow in confidence and begin to take giant steps. Students at the brink of disaster learn that their future lives are not dictated by their past. Students who are having difficulties with a particular subject have doors opened to them that were heretofore closed. Students who have thought of themselves as failures learn that they can succeed. Students who have hidden themselves away from others learn to become more social, more emotionally secure. Students who have been academically undernourished find school an exciting and meaningful place.

The gains may be hard to see at first; it takes courage and perseverance to keep at it. But once one has learned the art and the craft of the complex tasks of teaching, the payoffs are major, significant, and intensely rewarding. And that is why we do it.

Chapter 11

Endpaper

In Retrospect

Striving for mastery is what the best teachers do. The ugly truth is that such a goal is never fully realized; it is more a matter of moving in that direction, watching oneself in action, trying to figure out what you did that worked and what you did that failed to work, and making the appropriate adjustments when you face your class next. Sometimes it all goes well, and you come away from a teaching day exhilarated. Sometimes it goes badly, and you come away from a teaching day frustrated, disappointed, disillusioned. This is the "lot" of good teachers everywhere, at every teaching level.

Learning to teach is a lifelong process, making incremental changes in what one does each teaching day. Some, from outside the profession, may look at such challenges as making too rigorous demands. Others, from inside the profession, may see it as what it is: a matter of growing, learning, moving ahead, developing even more competence. In other words, never dull.

A PERSONAL JOURNEY

I came into the teacher education at the City University in New York by default. Becoming a teacher was not, initially, my consuming passion. I had begun my college studies with a business administration major but found the program lifeless. There were few other options open to me at the college; women were not, at that time, considered eligible candidates for a liberal arts degree and engineering was way out of my league. With few other options, I applied for and was admitted to the School of Education.

It wasn't until I started my student teaching practicum that I began to feel the joy for teaching, which has never left me. The headiness of being with a class of students was a revelation. The more I was in the classroom, the more I wanted to be there. Even then, in my professional virginity and hapless naiveté, I knew that it was important to treat students with kindness and respect. Even then, I knew that certain actions I saw my mentor teacher take were harmful and unhealthy for students' learning and self-esteem. Even though I didn't have the words yet to express those ideas, I knew in some deep inner place what teaching could and should be.

Taking a sequence of required "education courses" at the college was as much use to me as putting Band-Aids on a corpse. The lectures delivered by a cadre of tenured professors, long out of touch with the real life of the public schools, were dry, humorless, and heavy on "shoulds." We read tomes of history of education, educational psychology, and methods, but no attention was given to the application of these theories or methodologies to actual practice. My experience nil, my preparation wanting, my competence close to the zero mark on a ten-point scale, I nevertheless came into practice with a zeal that was unsupported by my know-how.

What I did have, however, was the experience of sitting in classrooms, as a student, watching and learning from those who taught me. And odd as it may sound, I learned more from my worst teachers; they gave me explicit lessons in how *not* to be a teacher.

My first-grade teacher was at the head of that class. She taught me about favorites. I was not one. She taught me about the misbehavior of children who talked in class. I was one. She taught me about keeping children at arm's length—she didn't want to get too close to any of us; we were the impoverished from neighborhood ghetto. She taught us that discipline meant humiliation and loss of self-esteem, both of which were diminishing. She taught me that even if you tried to please the teacher, unexpressed standards and expectations would kill your chances of being chosen for a part in the play.

She taught me that what I enjoyed most, reading, could be made excruciatingly painful when the same story was read orally, line by tortured line, up one row and down the other, until all meaning and pleasure had been extinguished. She taught me that truth had no place in responding to her questions: we were expected to tell her only what she wanted to hear.

Two years with her left such an imprint that I remember her still: the smell of the room, redolent of chocolate-covered graham crackers mixed with chalk dust, the bleak beige of unadorned walls, with only the black-and-white alphabet cards to divert the eye; the steam rising in staccato spurts from the vent on the radiator; the perfect handwriting on the blackboard; and the door with the little window offering a glimpse of the outside, where real life ran counterpart to our still-life experiences.

What I didn't know then was that her teaching would be pivotal in my own professional journey; my loathing of her was so intense that I could only become her antithesis.

My professional development journey began in my student teaching classroom, on the Lower East Side of New York City, where the first graders came with background stories that would murder any of their hopes of later success. I wanted to take them in my arms, comfort them, and soothe their hearts. Instead I put in my time, got a passing grade, a diploma, a NYC License to teach, and an open door to my own class.

While I recognized that I could not turn Charlie's mom away from drugs, Benno's dad from his criminal activities, Mary's hand-me-down clothes into elegant fashions, I nevertheless kept wanting to do just that: to make a difference so that children's lives could be happier, safer, more comfortable, easier.

It is toward those goals that I continued to strive all of my teaching life, to make a difference in the lives of my students so that they could reach for goals they wanted for themselves. I long ago gave up the quest for that "magic" that would make the totality of my teaching clear, answer all my questions, and prevent all problems from fracturing my students' lives. And eventually I learned to accept that even small steps paid off and that I was only a teacher engaged in my own struggle to learn.

I recognize that I cannot "right" all educational wrongs. I have grown comfortable with the realization that my students' struggles are what matter in shaping who they are and what they will become as adults. Such struggles must be part of each student's journey. What I can do is to recognize and appreciate each student's journey; continue to examine what I do, how I face each new class, how I use teacher-student interactions that enable, empower, and enrich their lives; and keep a constant check on what I must do to make that difference.

I'm taking an early morning flight to Chicago, and as the plane is boarding, I'm still grouchy from a 5:30 a.m. wake-up call, a restless night, long lines at the airport, and a dour-faced U.S. immigration officer who looks at my passport and studies my face as if I might be John Dillinger in drag. I'm relieved to settle myself, finally, into my aisle seat, take care to buckle my seatbelt, and put my book into the pocket of the seat in front of me. I settle back with a final glance out the window to the mountains of Vancouver, still covered with winter snow, although it is far into the spring. The man in the window seat smiles, and soon we begin to chat.

"What do you do?" he asks me.

"I'm a teacher," I tell him with a pride of purpose and position that has never left me. That I can still feel it, after all these years, makes me feel incredibly blessed. This teaching life has been well worth living.[1]

"Mastery is not something that strikes in an instant, like a thunderbolt, but in a gathering power that moves steadily through time, like weather" (Gardner, 1999).

NOTE

1. Adapted with permission. Reprinted by permission of the Publisher. From Selma Wassermann, *This Teaching Life: How I Taught Myself to Teach*. New York: Teachers College Press. Copyright © 2004 by Teachers College, Columbia University. All right reserved.

Appendix

Profiles of Teaching Competency
Form A: Pre-Service Professional Development

Selma Wassermann
Simon Fraser University
Burnaby, British Columbia
Wallace Eggert
Assistant Superintendent
Victoria Public Schools
Victoria, British Columbia
Copyright 1973 by Wassermann and Eggert
Revised 1986, 1988, 1994

PROFILES OF TEACHING COMPETENCY

What kinds of teacher behaviors are related to successful teaching? What kinds of characteristics do we see as important in the competent, effective, highly professional teacher?

This instrument identifies twenty behavioral profiles that are seen as related to competent classroom performance. These profiles do not include *everything* that a good teacher does. They do, however, represent what we consider to be some of the most important teaching functions that contribute to pupil learning.

Recommended in examining and assessing classroom functioning, this instrument is helpful in identifying teaching strengths and determining areas of needed professional growth.

DIRECTIONS

There are twenty pairs of behavioral profiles in this instrument. Each pair contains two views of a particular kind of teaching behavior—a "positive" view and a "negative" view.

As you study what the student teacher is doing in the classroom, observe how the behavior "lines up" with each particular pair of profiles. Then, rate the behavior observed according to the following scale:

Positive View:

Assign a rating of +5 if you observe these behaviors to be *clearly evident* in the student teacher's functioning. A rating of +5 suggests that this student teacher is an *outstanding example* of this profile.

Assign a rating of +3 or +4 if you observe these behaviors to be in evidence *some of the time*. A rating of +1 or +2 suggests that this student teacher reveals this behavior *from time to time*.

+5.....+4.....+3.....+2.....+1.....0....................

Negative View:

Assign a rating of −5 if you observe these behaviors to be *clearly evident* in the student teacher's functioning. A rating of −5 suggests that this student teacher is an *outstanding example* of this profile.

Assign a rating of −3 or −4 if you observe these behaviors to be *frequently evident* in the student teacher's functioning. A rating of −3 or −4 suggests that this student teacher is a *very good example* of this profile.

Assign a rating of −1 or −2 if you observe these behaviors to be evident *some of the time*. A rating of −1 or −2 suggests that this student teacher reveals this behavior *from time to time*.

....................0..... −1..... −2..... −3..... −4..... −5

"NO OP" ASSESSMENTS

In some cases, student teachers will not have had an opportunity to demonstrate some of these teaching behaviors. In these instances, a No Op rating should be used. No Op ratings are not negative assessments. For student teachers who are doing self-assessment, and who believe that they *might have* behaved in the way specified in the profile, but did not get a chance to do so, the appropriate rating is, nonetheless, No Op. Assessments are made on the basis of what is observed in performance, not on intent.

PLUS 5 ASSESSMENTS

The positive profiles in this instrument show what is considered to be the *highest level* of teaching ability. Consequently, +5 assessments would be those that reveal "teaching as art." Plus 5 assessments are given when the student teacher is seen to have consistently demonstrated the highest level of competency in that particular teaching function—a level reached after many years of classroom practice. Student teacher ratings are considered good when they have reached +3 and +4 levels.

What Do the Assessments Tell Us?

Assessments that are consistently rated at −5 would reveal classroom behavior considered to be negative. Student teachers who consistently obtain numerous −5 and −4 ratings are likely teaching in ways that are counterproductive to pupil learning.

Assessments at the −1, −2, and −3 levels identify those areas in which much growth is needed in order to promote effective classroom learning.

Assessments at the +1 and +2 levels identify those areas of functioning in which additional growth is needed in order to promote more effective classroom learning.

Assessments at the +3 level indicate that a student teacher's classroom behavior is competent in that area of professional functioning.

Promoting Professional Growth

Evaluating a teacher's classroom functioning is a difficult task. It is more difficult for the student teacher under scrutiny, who may be very anxious about the assessment and whose teaching may reflect that stress. It is also difficult for the classroom observer (school associate, faculty associate, etc.) who wants to ensure that the conditions of observation and the procedures used are both fair to the student teacher and reflective of that student's overall functioning.

Yet, without such scrutiny, without the opportunity of evaluating classroom functioning against clear standards of excellence, we have little hope of increasing competence and little chance of learning about which teaching skills require some additional development. We also lose the chance of knowing with some confidence about those professional functions in which some teachers are perceived to excel.

In order to promote more effective use of the profiles as a means of increasing opportunities for professional development, the following procedures are recommended:

1. Assessment of a student teacher's classroom functioning should be based on several visits to the classroom. This is necessary to ensure that the assessments reflect an overall perspective of the student teacher's functioning and not just a limited "one-shot" view that may not necessarily be representative of the fuller picture.
2. When the observer is making the assessment, the student teacher also rates himself or herself on the profiles. This self-evaluation is a critical aspect of the professional growth process.
3. Both observer and student teacher meet afterward to discuss their individual ratings on all the profiles. Where there is consistency in the ratings, the nature of the rating should dictate the discussion that follows. Where ratings are discrepant, this should provide rich opportunity for discussion about individual perceptions on that particular teaching function. When the ratings fall heavily into negative numbers, this should point clearly to areas of needed growth.
4. Before the conference concludes, it is imperative that specific plans are made for skill development in areas of needed growth. Without such explicit suggestions for growth, the exercise of evaluation itself is likely to lead more to frustration than it is to helpful, effective professional development.
5. It is recommended that the profiles be used at least twice during one student teaching semester and that they be used as formative evaluation procedures that are primarily concerned with professional development and increased teaching effectiveness.

SECTION I: TEACHER AS PERSON

1. Their Behavior Is Thoughtful

At the highest level, you would say that this student teacher's behavior is thoughtful. They act out of having considered alternatives; their choices for action are reasoned choices; their actions are appropriate to expressed goals. These student teachers seem to have a built-in monitoring system which aids them in analyzing their actions, and this analysis is based on objective criteria rather than on personal bias. You would be apt to conclude about these student teachers that they are "in touch" with what they are doing and what they do seems to have been considered and reflected upon with respect to their goals.

The antithesis of the thoughtful student teacher is one whose actions seem generated out of whim or caprice; their behavior is clearly inconsistent with expressed goals. These student teachers have not considered what to do before they do it; they do not appear to have considered alternatives; there seems to be a gap between what they say and what they do. When confronted with their actions, these student teachers may deny them ("I didn't do that!"), becoming increasingly defensive. The impression that these student teachers give is that they have not thought a lot about what they say or do.

RATING SCALE

+5 ..... +4 ..... +3 ..... +2 ..... +1 ..... 0 ..... −1 ..... −2 ..... −3 ..... −4 ..... −5 .....

Comments:

TEACHER AS PERSON

2. Their Behavior Is Self-initiating

At the highest level, you would say that these student teachers consistently take the initiative. They don't sit around and wait to be told; they don't need help at every step of the way. They are not afraid to take risks, to try things on their own. When their actions result in less than desirable ends, they are able to examine what has happened rationally, rather than considering it a personal defeat. When things don't work out well, they do not use it as an excuse to keep from trying again. Even in situations where resources are limited, they use what is available to make a start; they don't rationalize their inaction by saying that there aren't enough materials or that the materials are of the wrong type. You might say of these student teachers, "I can count on this person to take the initiative. He or she gets things done!"

The antithesis of the self-initiating student teacher is the one who waits to be told what to do. It's not that what they do is unsuccessful; it is that they rarely seize the opportunity to act on their own. Sometimes, they start out by doing something, but then they need to ask for help several times along the way. "Tell me what to do" and "What am I supposed to do?" and "What shall I do now?" characterizes their behavior. They may attempt to excuse their inaction by claiming that there aren't enough materials or that the materials aren't the right kind. They seem to have to depend on others to get them started.

RATING SCALE

+5 ..... +4 ..... +3 ..... +2 ..... +1 ..... 0 ..... −1 ..... −2 ..... −3 ..... −4 ..... −5 .....

Comments:

TEACHER AS PERSON

3. These Teachers Have a Clear Idea of What They Believe and Those Beliefs Guide Their Classroom Practices

At the highest level, you would find student teachers who have clear ideas of what they believe and whose classroom practices are consistent with those beliefs. In speaking with you, they give you the impression that they have thought a lot about their ideas; that is, the beliefs have been chosen after reflection. You can see that what they do is a reflection of those beliefs. There is a clarity about their purposes, about what they stand for. They come across as classroom practitioners with clear values, knowing where they are going and why. They know what they believe, and they believe in what they do.

At the other end of the scale are those whose actions are clearly inconsistent with their stated beliefs. They may say they believe in democracy in the classroom, but they are classic examples of authoritarian teachers. They may say they believe that teachers should have a voice in making decisions about what happens in the school, but they do not participate in committees or bother to exercise their votes, claiming that "what one person does doesn't really make a difference." Their actions and their expressed ideas are often so very far apart that what they do seems puzzling. Sometimes they rationalize what they do by saying, "They won't let me do that" or "They make me do that" to excuse actions that are inconsistent with expressed beliefs. However, when you ask them clarifying questions, their answers are evasive, or defensive, or inconsistent. It's hard to know what these student teachers *really* believe.

RATING SCALE

+5 ..... +4 ..... +3 ..... +2 ..... +1 ..... 0 ..... −1 ..... −2 ..... −3 ..... −4 ..... −5 .....

Comments:

TEACHER AS PERSON

4. They Are "Problem-Solvers"

At the highest level, you would see student teachers who, in the face of a difficult problem, would be able to identify the problem, suggest alternative courses of action, examine underlying assumptions, and propose workable strategies. In the face of conflicting data, these student teachers would "open their minds" to them and examine them with objectivity. You might say of them that in the presence of some new and complex problem, "they take the lead in planning the strategy." They are seen as inquiring, open-minded persons, able to function effectively in the face of new and complex problems.

The antithesis of the "problem-solving student teacher" is one who, in the face of a problem, seems to go to pieces. These student teachers don't know what to do or how to start. In the absence of some direction or leadership from others, they don't know where or how to begin. They seem unable to make a decision. They wait for others to start, and then they follow. They have much difficulty in entertaining discrepant data; their minds seem to be closed to them. Once embarked on a course of action, they are hard to budge. When new alternatives are introduced, they may say, "We already have a plan. Let's not waste any more time by fooling around with new ideas."

RATING SCALE

+5 ..... +4 ..... +3 ..... +2 ..... +1 ..... 0 ..... −1 ..... −2 ..... −3 ..... −4 ..... −5 .....

Comments:

TEACHER AS PERSON

5. They Can Put New Ideas Into Practice

At the highest level, these student teachers can take a new idea and put it into practice. They are able to make assessments of group needs, come up with an idea that is appropriate to those needs, and create a scheme for implementing the idea. They are not thwarted by limited resources; they seem to be able to do a lot with a little. They generate excitement about what they are doing. What they do is new and fresh, and there is a sense of life and vitality in their work.

On the other end of the scale, we find student teachers who apply rigid, formula approaches to most new situations. They seem to do the same things again and again, and they seem to do them in the same ways. They have difficulty seeing that a formula approach may be inappropriate to new situations; they are unable to create a new approach that is more relevant. They use what they already know and try to make that stick. They want specific and practical and "how to" kinds of help and have considerable difficulty in taking an educational principle and applying it in classroom practice. There is a staleness and lack of zest in what these teachers do in the classroom.

RATING SCALE

+5 ..... +4 ..... +3 ..... +2 ..... +1 ..... 0 ..... −1 ..... −2 ..... −3 ..... −4 ..... −5 .....

Comments:

TEACHER AS PERSON

6. You Can Rely On Them

At the highest level, you would find a person that you know you can depend on. If these student teachers say they are going to do something, you can depend on them to do it. If they are unable to fulfill a task, they find a way of communicating this in advance, so that other arrangements may be made. It is rare that these student teachers let you down. You feel a sense of trust in them, comfortable in the assurance that they will do what they say they are going to do.

The antithesis of the reliable student teacher is the one who cannot be counted upon. Again and again they offer to take on a task, and for one reason or another, they do not complete it. You have little faith in their ability to follow through, to do what they say they are going to do. In short, you know that if you needed a job done, you could not depend on them to do it.

RATING SCALE

+5 ..... +4 ..... +3 ..... +2 ..... +1 ..... 0 ..... −1 ..... −2 ..... −3 ..... −4 ..... −5 .....

Comments:

TEACHER AS PERSON

7. They Have a Positive Outlook

At the highest level, you would find a student teacher who has a cheerful, positive outlook on life. When things go wrong, they are not apt to attribute it to some manifest destiny. They take things in their stride. They smile and laugh a lot and seem genuinely to enjoy what they are doing. They have the capacity of looking at "the brighter side of life" and communicating this positive attitude to those who come in contact with them.

The antithesis of the student teacher with the positive outlook is the one who tends to see life in terms of blacks and shades of gray. They bitch and nag a lot about things that "never go right" and expend an unusual amount of time and energy in complaining. Sometimes, even after a situation is rectified, they want to talk about "how bad it was." "What's the use?" is typical of their negative attitude. They seem to infect others with their pessimism and with their bleak outlook on life.

RATING SCALE

+5 .....+4 .....+3 ..... +2 ..... +1 ..... 0 ..... −1 ..... −2 ..... −3 ..... −4 ..... −5 .....

Comments:

TEACHER AS PERSON

8. They Are "Reflective Practitioners"

At the highest level, these student teachers are thoughtful, intelligent observers of what goes on in the classroom. In situations of uncertainty, in situations where children behave in ways that are not immediately understood, they do not resort to simplistic explanations or judgmental labeling (e.g., "He's doing that because he's just lazy"). Rather they are able to size up and make sense of complex situations and risk self-initiated actions that seem appropriate to the situation. Their actions are thoughtfully and intelligently conceived—often representing new and original interventions that clearly fit. These student teachers' actions demonstrate a marriage of problem identification and problem solving.

In their problem-solving actions, they are able to watch themselves and watch the impact of their actions on the problem situation. This they do nondefensively—with an open attitude that allows for assessing the effect of their actions on the situation. They do not see their actions as ways to *solve the problem* once and for all. These student teachers understand that while others may help them, they are ultimately responsible for educating themselves through this process. For these student teachers, teaching is an "examined act," and in their ability to take risks to deal with problems creatively, they elevate teaching to an art.

At the other end of the scale are student teachers who adhere strictly to predetermined sets of procedures and apply them regardless of the need to assess each new classroom situation thoughtfully, on its own differential terms. Rather than making intelligent assessments of complex situations, they resort to simplistic explanations or judgmental labeling ("He's doing that because he's lazy"), seeing only what they wish to see and neglecting to probe for deeper, more complex meanings.

These student teachers have neglected *to see the problems*, and consequently they apply "wrong strategies" to deal with the situation. They are unaware of this mismatch between action and problem, chiefly because they have not learned *to watch*—to observe and make sense of what they see. Actions come out of convention instead of what is appropriate to the situation. When the action does not work, these teachers are likely to blame others for not responding as *they* should have done. When confronted with the inappropriateness of their action-on-problem, they respond defensively, unwilling to take a deeper look at how they themselves have misapplied strategies or misread the problem.

Because they have not learned to watch (either the situation or themselves in action), these student teachers have limited capability to learn from their own actions. They look for "packaged solutions" to problems and often look to others for those "solutions." If the "solution" does not work, they hold others to account instead of themselves. Teaching, for these student teachers, is an "unexamined act." There is no art to what they do.

RATING SCALE

+5 ..... +4 ..... +3 ..... +2 ..... +1 ..... 0 ..... −1 ..... −2 ..... −3 ..... −4 ..... −5 .....

Comments:

SECTION II: THE TEACHER AND THE KIDS: INTERACTIONS

9. They Prize, Care about Each Individual

At the highest level, you will find student teachers who allow their pupils to express their ideas, opinions, beliefs, and feelings and accept these without condemnation. Not only are they sensitive to and considerate of their pupils' feelings but communicate this sensitivity in ways the pupils can understand. "I am with you" is what is communicated to their students. In their interactions with them, their facial expressions, the tone of voice, and language give explicit evidence of warmth, praise, and encouragement. Their interactions reveal their close relationship with pupils, free of attempts to dominate them. After a brief interaction with these student teachers, pupils usually come away feeling a little better about themselves.

On the other end of the scale are those student teachers who show a lack of sensitivity to their pupils. In their interactions, they may appear indifferent rather than warm, disinterested rather than encouraging, mechanical rather than sincere in giving praise. They frequently reject the ideas and opinions of their pupils. Their criticisms are cutting and devaluing and seem to be made without regard to pupils' feelings. They don't seem to be able to understand how their pupils feel. In fact, they seem hardly to be aware that pupils' expressions of feeling have a place in the classroom.

RATING SCALE

+5 ..... +4 ..... +3 ..... +2 ..... +1 ..... 0 ..... −1 ..... −2 ..... −3 ..... −4 ..... −5 .....

Comments:

THE TEACHER AND THE KIDS: INTERACTIONS

10. They Know How to Observe, Diagnose, And Deal with Pupils with Behavioral Difficulties

At the highest level are student teachers who are able to make informed, intelligent observations of pupil behavior and use these as data to make diagnoses of problems that interfere with pupil learning. These diagnoses are then used to plan teaching strategies that are appropriate to the individual learner.

The observations made by these teachers are free from personal bias and value judgments. Behavioral descriptions are grounded in what has been observed. They do not label, condemn, attribute, or judge harshly. In describing behavior, these student teachers say, "This pupil did such and such" rather than "This pupil acted irresponsibly."

If a pupil needed special help, these student teachers would refer the pupil to the appropriate agency. While competent to act, they also recognize the limits of their own ability.

In short, these student teachers observe, interpret, and deal with pupil behavior in the most professional ways.

At the other end of the scale, you will find student teachers who see behavior that deviates from what they consider normal as "bad." Rather than attempting to unearth what lies behind such behavior, they are apt to attribute motives to the pupils (e.g., "She's just lazy," or, "He is not trying," or, "She doesn't want to learn"). Sometimes, these student teachers may try to explain the behavior in terms of their own arbitrary standards (e.g., "He behaves that way because he's an underachiever," or, "That's the way most of the non-academics act"). Once having "explained" the behavior, these student teachers will write the pupil off in terms of their own expectations.

These student teachers use punishment and other manipulative tactics as their chief tools for bringing about behavioral changes and advocate their use for bringing pupils into line.

RATING SCALE

+5 ..... +4 ..... +3 ..... +2 ..... +1 ..... 0 ..... −1 ..... −2 ..... −3 ..... −4 ..... −5 .....

Comments:

THE TEACHER AND THE KIDS: INTERACTIONS

11. They Use Reflective Responses to Help Pupils Think about What They Are Saying

At the highest level are student teachers who are skilled in using reflective responses as a means of helping pupils to examine their statements more thoughtfully. When pupils express ideas, thoughts, beliefs, these student teachers use responses that enable pupils to become clearer in their own thinking. Reflective responses are used to help pupils "work" their ideas and assume responsibility for those ideas.

These student teachers are able *to hear* the pupils' ideas, and they are able *to attend* to the nuances of pupils' expressions. They are able to formulate appropriate reflective responses—knowing when to reflect basically what is being said, when to paraphrase, and when to interpret the pupils' ideas. Whichever reflective response is used, the tone is always nonjudgmental, conveying respect for the pupil *and* for the idea.

These student teachers are able to use reflective interactions in ways that help pupils to find deeper and more substantive meanings in the curriculum being studied.

At the other end of the scale are those student teachers who are overly directive. Their practices include manipulating their pupils to agree with their own ideas. They are expert at maneuvering them into producing the "right" response. "Wouldn't you like to empty the basket, Peter?" and "Isn't that right, boys and girls?" are typical of their responses to their pupils. Instead of using reflective responding, they are given to arguing. The intention is not to help pupils to think about their own ideas but rather to bring pupils' ideas more into line with their own.

Misuse of reflective responding is another form of antithetical behavior. In their attempts to be nonauthoritarian, these student teachers will almost never be directive, even when the situation demands direction. In the extreme, such a student teacher would ask a clarifying question when life and limb are at stake, rather than take a directive stance. Reflective responding is used indiscriminately in responding to pupils, rather than as a means for helping pupils think about issues of substance.

RATING SCALE

+5 ..... +4 ..... +3 ..... +2 ..... +1 ..... 0 ..... −1 ..... −2 ..... −3 ..... −4 ..... −5 .....

Comments:

THE TEACHER AND THE KIDS: INTERACTIONS

12. They Promote Pupils' Thinking

At the highest level you will find student teachers who are skilled in promoting the thinking of their pupils. The questions they choose to ask pupils are concerned with the higher cognitive skills of interpreting data, problem solving, applying principles, and generating new principles, rather than with the recall of factual information. You will hear these teachers ask more questions like, "Do you have any idea of why that might be so?" and "What might be another explanation?" and "How can we go about deciding which one of these is correct?" rather than questions like, "In which year was metal first discovered?" and "What were the three causes of the French Revolution?"

These student teachers wait for the pupils to respond to the questions. They give pupils time to think. It is clear that such student teachers are interested in many possible explanations and answers, rather than in finding a single, correct answer. Instead of doing pupils' thinking for them, these student teachers invite the pupils to think for themselves. They value the development of inquiry in their pupils, and this emphasis permeates their classrooms.

At the opposite end of the scale are student teachers who place the highest value on the acquisition of information for the purpose of arriving at the single, correct answer. Their questions to pupils are primarily of the recall-of-information type. They believe that their primary job is to get the students to learn the information for that grade. In their interactions with pupils, these student teachers rarely give them time to think through things. They seem to be in a race with the clock to get across as much content as possible. They give the impression that it is the student teacher who is doing most of the thinking in that class and maybe that's the way these student teachers really want it.

RATING SCALE

+5 ..... +4 ..... +3 ..... +2 ..... +1 ..... 0 ..... –1 ..... –2 ..... –3 ..... –4 ..... –5 .....

Comments:

THE TEACHER AND THE KIDS: INTERACTIONS

13. There's a Lot of Interaction among Pupils In Their Classes

At the highest level you will find student teachers who encourage and invite much interaction among their pupils. Their classrooms seem to be beehives, where there is an almost constant flow of pupil-to-pupil conversation, as the pupils actively engage in learning. These teachers may interject questions such as "What do you think about that, Harlow?" and "What are some of your ideas, Perry?" to promote further inquiry and to increase pupil responses. You get the impression that the focus in these classes is on the pupils. There's a lot of purposeful pupil activity, pupil inquiry, and exchange of ideas. These student teachers provide many kinds of curriculum experiences in which pupils engage in cooperative learning—discussing together and learning from one another.

These teachers do not cast themselves in the role of dispensers of information. They recognize that pupil interaction and cooperative learning are important dimensions of teaching.

At the other end of the scale are student teachers who "talk all the time." They believe that everything they say is important, and they insist that students are quiet in their classrooms for most class sessions. They see their main role as imparting information, following through by questioning pupils to see if they have been listening. These student teachers are the dominant people in their classrooms. If they were to step out of the room for a moment, the class would fall apart. They may permit their pupils to talk with each other occasionally, as a recreational activity, but rarely in the context of what they consider a teaching–learning experience.

RATING SCALE

+5 ..... +4 ..... +3 ..... +2 ..... +1 ..... 0 ..... –1 ..... –2 ..... –3 ..... –4 ..... –5 .....

Comments:

THE TEACHER AND THE KIDS: INTERACTIONS

14. These Student-Teachers Are Real People to Their Pupils

At the highest level you will find student teachers who respond to pupils with genuineness. In their interactions with pupils they are "themselves"—not role-playing, distant professionals. There is no doubt that they really mean what they say. When a pupil approaches these student teachers with a problem, they don't intellectualize. They are unafraid to say, "I don't know."

When confronted with pupils' difficult behavior, these teachers respond without defensiveness. Their reactions are honest and open. The message conveyed by them in their interactions with pupils is that they are authentic.

At the opposite end of the scale are student teachers who put on a professional mask in their interactions with pupils. When pupils discuss concerns that affect them deeply, these student teachers become uncomfortable. They respond by intellectualizing. Their interactions come across as phony. They become extremely defensive in the presence of pupils' challenging behavior. The message conveyed by these student teachers is that you don't really know the real person behind the facade.

RATING SCALE

+5 ..... +4 ..... +3 ..... +2 ..... +1 ..... 0 ..... −1 ..... −2 ..... −3 ..... −4 ..... −5 .....

Comments:

SECTION III:

The Teacher, the Kids, And the "Stuff": Classroom Life

15. They Know What They Are Doing In the Classroom, And It Makes Sense

At the highest level are student teachers who are skillful in what they are doing in the classroom. Their teaching strategies and the curriculum materials they use are appropriate to their educational goals. They are able to describe what they are doing and why they are doing it in a clear and educationally sound way. They generate feelings of confidence in what is happening in their classrooms.

At the other end of the scale are student teachers who seem to be teaching "off the cuff." You get the impression that they are making it up as they go along, that they really haven't thought much about what they are doing. When questioned about what is happening in their classrooms, they become very defensive and try to rationalize what they are doing by making up objectives to justify the actions. These student teachers may work hard, but they can't seem to "get it to come right." There doesn't seem to be a close connection between their teaching strategies, their choice of curriculum materials, and their stated goals. What happens in their classrooms doesn't seem to make sense in terms of what is educationally sound.

RATING SCALE

+5 ..... +4 ..... +3 ..... +2 ..... +1 ..... 0 ..... −1 ..... −2 ..... −3 ..... −4 ..... −5 .....

Comments:

THE TEACHER, THE KIDS, AND THE "STUFF": CLASSROOM LIFE

16. They Are Knowledgeable In Their Fields

At the highest level, these student teachers exhibit broad and deep knowledge of the curriculum, of principles of learning, and of human growth and development as these relate to their levels of teaching. If these student teachers specialize in a particular subject area, they are at home in it. They are well informed and they have read extensively. There is an intellectual depth to their discussions with their colleagues, and their work in the classroom reflects this knowledge of the field. When they explain something to a pupil, or to a colleague, they are able to make themselves clearly understood. They recognize the limits of their knowledge, and where they are uninformed, they admit it. Their knowledge earns our respect.

At the opposite end of the scale is the student teacher who is uninformed. They lack know-how in their field. If they have read the literature in their field, they do not indicate it, either in their discussions with their colleagues or in the quality of their teaching. Their explanations to pupils are unclear. You wonder if they themselves really understand what they are saying. Their inconsistency, the shallowness of their presentations, and their attempts to disguise their limited understanding indicate their lack of knowledge in their field.

RATING SCALE

+5 ..... +4 ..... +3 ..... +2 ..... +1 ..... 0 ..... −1 ..... −2 ..... −3 ..... −4 ..... −5 .....

Comments:

THE TEACHER, THE KIDS, AND THE "STUFF": CLASSROOM LIFE

17. They Use Evaluation to Promote Learning

At the highest level are student teachers who use evaluation to obtain data for promoting further learning. They recognize that evaluation is highly subjective, and they are undogmatic and open-minded about using the results. They recognize the difference between evaluation and grading, and they use evaluation as a way of helping students to learn. These student teachers use many different kinds of evaluation procedures, but whatever procedure is used is carefully chosen and is appropriate to stated goals. Moreover, when they engage in evaluation of their pupils' work, there is a sound purpose for the evaluation. The methods of evaluation do not in any way diminish the dignity of the pupil. Evaluations include suggestions for improvement and these are communicated to the pupils. These teachers exhibit a concern about promoting self-evaluation in pupils and provide for self-evaluative experiences in their classrooms.

Antithetically, you will find student teachers who are primarily concerned with *how much* the pupils have learned and with grading them accordingly. They believe that grading is objective and that pupils' learning can be assessed objectively. Frequently, these student teachers are dogmatic about test results and use these and grades in a punitive way. They operate on the theory that pupils are motivated to learn by failure, and they may use the threat of failure as a device to promote learning. Their evaluative procedures usually take the form of short-answer and essay-type tests, and they rarely communicate to pupils concrete ideas for improvement. Catch phrases such as "careless spelling" and "try harder" and "good" pass for suggestions to promote learning. The main purpose for evaluation in these student teachers' classes is to arrive at a grade. If pupils fail, it is because "they are just not capable of doing the work."

RATING SCALE

+5 ..... +4 ..... +3 ..... +2 ..... +1 ..... 0 ..... –1 ..... –2 ..... –3 ..... –4 ..... –5 .....

Comments:

THE TEACHER, THE KIDS, AND THE "STUFF": CLASSROOM LIFE

18. The Classroom Is a Vital, Alive, And Zestful Place

At the highest level are student teachers who have made their classrooms alive and vital places for learning. There seems to be a lot of activity going on and it is purposeful activity. There is evidence around the room of pupils' work, and you can see that pupils have been and are engaged in challenging activities. These student teachers continually bring fresh ideas into the classroom, and they initiate curriculum experiences that have meaning and relevance for the lives of the students. They provide for individual choice, pacing and cooperative learning in most curriculum activities. The time in these classes passes quickly and the pupils are sorry to hear the bell ring. These classes are intense, stimulating, and vital places and it is exciting to be in them.

Antithetically, you will find student teachers whose classrooms are boring and tedious places. More often than not, all the pupils are doing the same work at the same time. When one pupil finishes early, he or she must wait for the rest of the class to finish. Much emphasis is placed on reading from the text, doing worksheets, or answering questions from the blackboard. When there is group discussion, the topic may be unimaginative or trivial, and the pupils seem to be too bored to participate. The apathy in these classrooms is usually attributed to pupils who "don't care." These teachers don't recognize that it is they who are uninspiring and humdrum. When the recess or lunch bell sounds, pupils explode out of these classes. One hour in these rooms seems like a year.

RATING SCALE

+5 ..... +4 ..... +3 ..... +2 ..... +1 ..... 0 ..... −1 ..... −2 ..... −3 ..... −4 ..... −5 .....

Comments:

THE TEACHER, THE KIDS, AND THE "STUFF": CLASSROOM LIFE

19. The Teaching Materials Used Are Varied, Imaginative, And Relevant

At the highest level you will find student teachers who use a wide variety of resources as teaching materials. In an elementary classroom, you will find a good supply of arts and crafts materials, library books, paperbacks, magazines, photographs, science equipment, concrete mathematical materials, and newspapers. In a secondary classroom, many different kinds of materials are available that are relevant to the subject matter of the class. These student teachers may use field trips, videos, films, and recordings as part of the curriculum. Visitors are invited to the class as resource people. Pupils engage with learning materials in "hands-on" and "minds-on" ways. Materials created and developed by the student teachers contribute to pupils' thinking about what is important in the curriculum. Materials reflect the deeper, more substantive curriculum issues—the "big ideas"—rather than the trivialities. These teachers have created rich learning environments in their classrooms through their selection and development of a large and varied learning materials resource.

At the other end of the scale, you will find student teachers who use a very limited range of classroom materials. Major emphasis is placed on the use of textbooks, library reference books, and workbooks. Classroom walls may provide no stimulus to thought. They may be empty or adorned with old posters expressing banal sentiments and patterned art work. Very little use is made of curriculum materials in the arts or the rich "stuff" of other curriculum areas. Pupils have little opportunity to touch or handle materials. Curriculum experiences in this classroom are mostly of the paper-and-pencil and textbook type.

RATING SCALE

+5 ..... +4 ..... +3 ..... +2 ..... +1 ..... 0 ..... −1 ..... −2 ..... −3 ..... −4 ..... −5 .....

Comments:

THE TEACHER, THE KIDS, AND THE "STUFF": CLASSROOM LIFE

20. These Teachers Unify Their Groups

At the highest level, these student teachers have succeeded in the development of harmonious working groups in their classrooms. The pupils seem to appreciate each other; they have respect for each other, and the morale in the class seems unusually high. The class seems to have pride in itself as a group; what's more, pupils seem to be very productive, working together like a team. These teachers have contributed to the development of group unity by assuring that each pupil has had an opportunity to earn status and respect in the group; by providing the opportunity for pupils to get to know each other; by prizing the different skills that different pupils have to offer; and by creating a climate in the classroom that helps every learner to feel secure, prized, cared about, and accepted.

At the other end of the scale, you will find student teachers who are not concerned with group morale. If they are concerned, they do not seem to know how to bring it about. In the classrooms of these teachers, the pupils may seem downright rude to each other. There may be a lot of bickering and nagging and fighting. These classes do not seem to be "groups" at all. There is no sense of camaraderie, no *esprit de corps*, no real feeling of respect of one pupil for another. These student teachers contribute to this discontent by openly criticizing pupils, by being intolerant of other than academic skills, by having "favorites" and "victims," by "picking" on certain pupils, and by generally showing a lack of respect for their students. These classrooms are not security-giving but intimidating. These student teachers generate fear rather than acceptance. Their pupils dislike school, and their interactions with each other are hostile and subtractive.

RATING SCALE

+5 ..... +4 ..... +3 ..... +2 ..... +1 ..... 0 ..... −1 ..... −2 ..... −3 ..... −4 ..... −5 .....

Comments:

Bibliography

Aiken, Wilford M. (1943). *Thirty Schools Tell Their Story.* New York, NY: Harper & Brothers.
Appiah, Kwame Anthony. (2020). "The Ethicist." *New York Times,* January 5, pp. 18–19.
Ashton-Warner, Sylvia. (1963). *Teacher.* New York, NY: Simon & Schuster.
Barham, James A. and Thomas, Alex. (2019). "Jaime Escalante in the 21st Century: Still Standing and Delivering." *The Quad.* www.thebest schools.org/magazine.
Bianco, Margaret Williams. (1958). *The Velveteen Rabbit.* New York, NY: Doubleday.
Brammer, Lawrence M. (1979). *The Helping Relationship.* Englewood, NJ: Prentice Hall.
Brown, Mary and Precious, Norman. (1968). *The Integrated Day in the Primary School.* London: Ward Lock.
Carkhuff, Robert. (1969). *Helping and Human Relations, Vol. 1.* New York, NY: Holt, Rinehart and Winston.
Carkhuff, Robert and Berenson, David H. (1983). *The Skilled Teacher.* Amherst, MA: Human Resources Development Press.
Costa, Arthur. (ed.) (1985). *Developing Minds. A Resource Book for Teaching Thinking.* Alexandria, VA: ASCD.
Cuban, Larry. (1982). "Persistent Instruction: The High School Classroom, 1900-1980." *Phi Delta Kappan,* 64, 113–18.
Dewey, John. (1916). *Democracy and Education.* New York, NY: Macmillan.
Dollard, John, (1939). *Frustration and Aggression.* New Haven, CT: Yale University Press.
Dunbar, Flanders. (1948). *Mind and Body: Psychomatic Medicine.* New York, NY: Random House.
Durm, Mark. (1993). "An A Is Not an A Is Not an A: A History of Grading." *The Educational Forum,* 57, pp. 294–98.

Finkelstein, Isadore E. (1913). "The Marking System in Theory and Practice." *Educational Psychology Monographs*, p. 10.
Fleming, Robert S. (1951). "Psychomatic Illness and Emotional Needs." *Educational Leadership*, November, 1951.
Freedman, Samuel G. (1990). *Small Victories. The Real World of a Teacher, Her Students, and Their High School*. New York, NY: Harper & Row.
Friere, Paulo. (1983). *Pedagogy of the Oppressed*. New York, NY: Continuum.
Gardner, John. (1999). *On Becoming a Writer*. New York, NY: W.W. Norton.
Gazda, George. (1973). *Human Relations Development*. Boston, MA: Allyn & Bacon.
Gordon, Thomas. (1974). *Teacher Effectiveness Training*. New York, NY: P. H. Wyden.
Greenberg, Leslie S. and Johnson, Nancy E. (1978). "Towards a More Authentic Teacher." *Teacher Education*, October, pp. 74–83.
Gullette, Margaret Morganroth. (1982). *The Art and Craft of Teaching*. Boston, MA: Harvard-Danforth Center for Teaching and Learning.
Harris, Albert J. (1990). *How to Increase Reading Ability: A Guide to Developmental and Remedial* Methods, 9th ed. London: Longmans Publishing Group.
Howes, Virgil. (1974). *Informal Teaching in the Open Classroom*. New York, NY: Macmillan.
Ibarra, Herminia. (2015). "The Authenticity Paradox." Boston: *Harvard Business Review*, Jan–Feb. issue.
Jourard, Sidney. (1964). *The Transparent Self*. New York, NY: Van Nostrand.
Kamill, Constance. (1980). *Group Games in Early Education*. Washington, DC: National Association for the Education of Young Children.
Kamill, Constance. (1994). *Young Children Continue to Reinvent Arithmetic*. New York, NY: Teachers College Press.
Kveton, Adam. (2017). "SD 69 Students Build and Share Video Games." *Parksville Qualicum Beach News*, May 31, 2017.
Leahy, Robert. (2009). *Authentic Educating*. Lanham, MD: University Press of America.
Levine, Arthur. (2006). "Educating School Teachers." *The Education Schools Project*. Princeton, NJ: The Woodrow Wilson National Fellowship Foundation.
Levine, Madeline. (2020). *Ready or Not: Preparing Our Kids to Thrive in an Uncertain and Rapidly Changing World*. New York, NY: HarperCollins.
Meister, Denise G. and Jenks, Charles. (2012). "Making the Transition from Preservice to Inservice Teaching: Beginning Teachers' Reflections." Published online: https://doi.org/10.1080/01626620.2000.10463014.
Molnar, Alex. (2019). "Virtual Schools in the U.S. 2019, Executive Summary." *Education Policy Center*. Boulder, Colorado.
Moustakas, Clark. (1966). *The Authentic Teacher*. Cambridge, MA: Howard A. Doyle.
Murphy, Kate. (2020). "Lessons in the Lost Art of Listening." *New York Times*, January 12, 2020.
Paul, Richard and Elder, Linda. (2002). *Critical Thinking: Tools for Taking Charge of Your Learning and Your Life*. Saddle River, NJ: Pearson.

Pogrow, Stanley. (2005). "HOTS Revisited: A Thinking Development Approach to Reducing the Learning Gap After Grade 3." *Phi Delta Kappan*, 87(1), 64–75.

Raths, Louis E. (1998). *Meeting the Needs of Children: Creating Security and Trust.* Troy, NY: Educator's International Press, Inc.

Raths, Louis E. and Burrell, Anna. (1963). *Understanding the Problem Child.* West Orange, NJ: The Economics Press.

Raths, Louis E., Harmin, Merrill, and Simon, Sidney B. (1978). *Values and Teaching. Working with Values in the Classroom,* 2nd ed. Columbus, OH: Charles Merrill.

Raths, Louis E., Wassermann, Selma, Jonas, Arthur, and Rothstein, Arnold. (1966). *Teaching for Thinking: Theory, Strategies and Activities for the Classroom.* Columbus, OH: Charles E. Merrill.

Raths, Louis E., Wassermann, Selma, Jonas, Arthur, and Rothstein, Arnold. (1986). *Teaching for Thinking: Theory, Strategies and Activities for the Classroom,* 2nd ed. New York, NY: Teachers College Press.

Ravitch, Diane. (2020). *Slaying Goliath: The Passionate Resistance to Privatization and the Fight to Save America's Schools.* New York, NY: Knopf.

Roblyer, M. D. and Hughes, Joan E. (2018). *Integrating Educational Technology into Teaching,* 8th ed. New York, NY: Pearson.

Rogers, Carl. (1961). *On Becoming a Person.* Boston: Houghton Mifflin.

Rogers, Carl and Steven, Barry. (1967). *Person to Person: The Problem of Being Human.* Walnut Creek, CA: Real People Press.

Rubin, Louis D. Jr. (ed.) (1987). *An Apple for My Teacher.* Chapel Hill, NC: Algonquin Books.

Segal, Judith, Chipman, Susan, and Glaser, Robert. (1985). *Thinking and Learning Skills, Volumes 1 and 2.* Hillsdale, NJ: Lawrence Erlbaum.

Sternberg, Robert J. (1987). "Teaching Critical Thinking: Eight Easy Ways to Fail Before You Begin." *Phi Delta Kappan*, 68(6), 456–59.

Truax, Charles B. and Mitchell, Kevin M. (1971). "Research on Certain Therapist Interpersonal Skills in Relation to Process and Outcome." In Bergin and Garfield (eds.), *Handbook of Psychotherapy and Behavior Change: An Empirical Analysis.* New York, NY: John Wiley and Sons, pp. 299–344.

Wassermann, Selma. (1986). "Beliefs and Personal Power: The Difference Between a Chairperson and a Charperson IS How She Behaves." *College Teaching*, 34(2), Spring, 1996, pp. 69–74.

Wassermann, Selma. (1994). *Introduction to Case Method Teaching.* New York, NY: Teachers College Press.

Wassermann, Selma. (2000). *Serious Players in the Primary Classroom.* New York, NY: Teachers College Press.

Wassermann, Selma. (2009). *Teaching for Thinking Today: Theory, Strategies and Activities for the K-8 Classroom.* New York, NY: Teachers College Press.

Wassermann, Selma. (2017). "Changing Course: Re-Thinking Teacher Education Course Design." *Childhood Education*, 93, pp. 346–55.

Wassermann, Selma and Eggert, Wallace. (1976). "Profiles of Teaching Competency: A Way of Looking at Classroom Teaching Performance." *Canadian Journal of Education*, 1(1), pp. 67–73.

Wassermann, Selma and Eggert, Wallace. (1973, 1986, 1988, 1994). *Profiles of Teaching Competency*. Burnaby: Simon Fraser University, Faculty of Education.

Wassermann, Selma and Ivany, J. W. George. (1996). *The New Teaching Elementary Science: Who's Afraid of Spiders?* New York, NY: Teachers College Press.

Wentworth, Nancy, Earle, Rodney, and Connell, Michael. (2004, 2010, 2015). *Integrating Information Technology in the Teacher Education Curriculum: Process and Products of Change*. New York, NY: Routledge.

Zeichner, Kenneth M. (2018). *The Struggle for the Soul of Education*. New York, NY: Routledge.

Index

activity: hands-on group activity, 86; innovative methods, 83; professional-day workshops, 83; "tried-and-true" methods, 84
anxiety, 32
An Apple for My Teacher (Rubin), 94
Ashton-Warner, Sylvia, 87
assessment tools, 73–75
assignments, 6
attending, defined, 45

beginning teachers: managing behavior, 6; parents and professionals, conflicts with, 6; teacher education, 6–7; time constraints, 6; work overload, 6
beliefs, 17, 105

Camrose, 43
children's performance, 86
classroom: counterproductive behavior, 29; management, 6; practices, 83; quality of life, 44; record keeping, 30; student's behavior, 29; working groups in, 123
classroom teachers, 42
competency, teaching, 99
counter-productive behaviors, 29, 32
curriculum, 7, 83; designing, 91; experiences, 121; framework, 64, 67–70, 75; and IT, 58–60; materials, xx, 118; task, 35–36

debriefing, 66
decision-making: curriculum experiences, 3; judgment and knowledge, 4; skill and intuition, 4; students' written and oral work, 3
Dewey, John, 57
Dunbar, Flanders, 31

educational goals, 118
educational practice, 85
Eggert, Wallace, 12
elementary classroom, 122
emotional health, 41
emotional needs: students, 30–32; teaching strategies, 32–34
emotional problems, 28
evaluation, 120
Executive Order 1066, 59

facilitative skills, 55
Fadiman, Dorothy, 71
Fleming, Robert S., 31

genuineness, 20–22
Golden High School, 62–63
Google, 59

group discussions, 85
group morale, 123
group unity, 123

impediments to learning, 38
intelligent decisions, 4
intelligent thinking, 35
interactive process, 3
interactive skills, 42
interpersonal skills, 45

Joe, 28, 87
Jourard, Sidney, 20

Kamill, Constance, 38
King George VI, 93
knowledge, 119

learning: behavior impediments, 38; evaluation, 120; materials, 122; problems, 6; profiles, xx; social and emotional learning, 59
Lee, Mai, 77, 78
Levine, Arthur, 7, 28
listening skills, 44
Logue, Lionel, 94

materials, xx, 122
math education, 38
meetings, 4
mental health, 9
Mitchell, Kevin M., 28
Molnar, Alex, 63
Murphy, Kate, 44

No Op ratings, 100

parent-teacher conferences, 80
physical health, 24
physical problems, 28
Plus 5 assessments, 101
presentations, 119
problem-solving, 18–19, 106
professional development program, 87
professional growth, 101–2

pupils' challenging behavior, 117
pupils' feelings, 112
pupils' thinking, 115
pupil-to-pupil conversation, 116

Qualicum Beach Elementary School, 60–62

Raths, Louis E., 30, 34
Ravitch, Diane, 74
reading disability, 38
response: analysis of ideas, 48–49; challenge, 49–52; feelings and personal concerns, 46; reflective response, 46–48, 114; students' expression of feelings, 52–54

school boards, 92
secondary classroom, 122
self-confidence, 22–24
self-esteem, 42
self-evaluations, 79–80
self-initiating, 104
Semmelweiss, Ludwig, 84
skills: apprehending, 46; attending, 46; cognitive skills, 34; debriefing, 66; higher-order thinking skills, 34; interactive skills, 42; interpersonal skills, 45; listening, 44, 45, 46; problem-solving skills, 18–19
social learning problems, 28
STREAM program, 60
stress, 32
student engagement, 71
students, 66; aggressiveness, 31; assignments and tests, 80; behavior problem, 4; cognitive skills, 34; competence, 80; confidence of, 74; counterproductive behaviors, 34; difficulties, 76–77; dysfunctional behaviors, 38; emotional needs, 30–31; funding and professional resources for, xix; higher-order thinking skills, 34; ideas, 70; learning difficulties, 29; physical

and emotional burdens, xix; psychosomatic symptoms of illness, 31; quality of learning, xx; self-esteem, 42; self-evaluations, 79–80; self-initiating student teacher, 103; submissiveness, 31; teacher's behavior, 103; thinking skills, 34; withdrawing behavior, 31
Summers, Harry, 6

Teacher (Ashton-Warner), 87
teacher-centered lectures, 6
teacher education: assignments, 6; behavior problems, 6; classroom management, 6; curriculums, 7; hands-on student involvement, 6; learning problems, 6; list of "to-dos," 6; skills and knowledge, 7; teacher-centered lectures, 6; teaching skills, 7
teacher-parent conferences, 80
teachers: ability, 66; beginning teachers. *See* beginning teachers; challenge, 28; clarity of beliefs, 17; components, 15; decisions, 16; educational experiences, 16; feedback, 77–79; fundamental beliefs, 17; genuineness, 20–22; growth, 16; innovative classroom methods, 85; judgments, 74; physical health, 24; problem-solving skills, 18–19; professional functioning, 4; professional tasks, xx; self-confidence, 22–24; self-initiating student teacher, 103; values, 17
teachers' decision-making. *See* decision-making

teacher-student interactions, 3, 97, 112; behavioral changes, 113; behavioral descriptions, 113; classroom discussions, xx; facilitative skills, 55; punishment and manipulative tactics, 113; pupil learning, 113; teaching strategies, 113
teaching behavior, 100
teaching competence, 99; behavioral characteristics, 12; categories of, 13–14; profiles of, 12–13
teaching goals, xx, 8
teaching materials, 92
teaching methods, xx
teaching skills, 7
teaching strategies, 118; activities, 37; curriculum task, 35–36; debriefing, 37; investigative play group, 36–37; lack of experience with thinking, 35–37; special teacher, 30
Tesla, 84
time constraints, 6
"tried-and-true" methods, 84

virtual schools, 63

Wassermann, Selma, 12
Wikipedia, 59
William, 43
work overload, 6
workshops, 4
World War II, 94
Wright Brothers, 84
written exercise, 74
written materials, xx

Zeichner, Kenneth M., 7

About the Author

Selma Wassermann is professor emerita in the Faculty of Education at Simon Fraser University and holder of the University Award for Teaching Excellence. Her books include *Evaluation Without Tears* (2020), *Teaching in the Age of Disinformation* (2018), *What's the Right Thing to Do?* (2019), *Teaching for Thinking Today* (2009), *This Teaching Life* (2004), *The Art of Interactive Teaching* (2017), and *An Introduction to Case Method Teaching: A Guide to the Galaxy* (1994).

www.ingramcontent.com/pod-product-compliance
Lightning Source LLC
Chambersburg PA
CBHW022015300426
44117CB00005B/203